Six Steps from Eden

An Engaging Exploration
into the Creation, Temptation,
and the Fall of Mankind

by Michael J. Torrence

Dedicated to my wife Cathy, who has been my faithful partner in life and ministry for the past 38 years.

To my Sons and Daughter-In-Laws and my Grandchildren, you are my greatest blessings.

To my friends, who with great patience, prayerfully encouraged me.

To my extended family of Heartsway Baptist Church who I am privileged to serve.

And to my God and Heavenly Father who has graciously and patiently permitted this book.

Every good gift and every perfect gift is from above,
and comes down from the Father of lights, with whom
there is no variation or shadow of turning.

Of His own will He brought us forth by the word of truth, that we
might be a kind of first fruits of His creatures. (James 1:17,18)

...and from Jesus Christ, the faithful witness, the firstborn from
the dead, and the ruler over the kings of the earth. To Him who
loved us and washed us from our sins in His own blood, and
has made us kings and priests to His God and Father, to Him
be glory and dominion forever and ever. Amen. (Rev.1:5,6)

Contents

Preface

Written in parallel with the Holy Scriptures, "Six Steps from Eden" explores mysteries surrounding creation, temptation, and the fall of mankind.

The Biblical book of Genesis is a book of beginnings. It is the summary of how everything that is came to be. While the Bible itself is obscure in many ways, it does provide definitive answers to some of life's most important questions such as: Does God exist? Where did we come from? How did we get here? Why are we here?

This book begins with the fundamental truths of God's Word and presents what could have been said and how some things, left unrevealed, may have transpired. Woven into the fabric of what is gleaned from the Bible, an allegory of truth emerges. Presented in an engaging story that parallels the Biblical book of Genesis, great care has been taken to preserve the original revelation and intention of the stories. No fictitious characters have been created. Creative liberty has been exercised only in the areas where a rational and reasonable hypothesis may be considered.

God, using His Word alone, created all things with the intentional purpose of revealing Himself through creation to those He has created.

"*The Heavens declare the glory of God;And the firmament shows His handiwork.*" Psalms 19:1 Diligently read the Bible as it wonderfully reveals and describes the Glory of the Creator.

It is my hope that this book will produce for the reader a desire to dig deeper into the Bible itself and develop a closer relationship with the One True God who has established and created all things for that very purpose. "*God is a rewarder to those who diligently seek Him.*" Hebrews 11:6

The contents of this work should in no way be considered adding to or further completing the already Perfect Inspired Word of God. "Six Steps from Eden" is simply a prayerful exploration into the exciting possibilities of what in this life can only be vaguely imagined, but once in the presence of God will forever be clearly understood.

Someday, thanks be to Jesus Christ our Lord, those who have believed upon Jesus Christ and received the gift of salvation, will experience new life in the presence of His Glory forever!

"*When that which is perfect is come, then that which is in part shall be done away.*" "*For now, we see through a glass darkly; but then face to face: now I know in part; but then shall I know even as also I am known."* 1Corinthians 13:10,12

To God be the Glory!

Introduction

nyone who has ever served in youth ministries can affirm at some point the children will ask this question, "Where did God come from?" To explain His eternal existence, having no beginning and no ending is a daunting task. This question falls into the category of requiring nothing less than faith to believe that He has always been. The next reasonable question that usually follows is "What is Faith?" So then faith itself must be explained. Thankfully, in most cases, children are the most willing to accept by faith what we cannot fully explain.

While the Bible gives us much revelation to help us understand and answer these questions, there are some things simply not revealed in the Bible and it takes the willing, undoubting faith like a child to simply trust and believe. The Biblical book of Genesis is a book of beginnings. It is the summary of how everything that is came to be. While the Bible itself is obscure in many ways, it does provide definitive answers to some of life's most important questions such as: Does God exist? Where did we come from? How did we get here? Why are we here?

One of the things we know from the Bible concerning the question of the origin of God is that God exists eternally. We see this in many places in the Bible and here are a few, Rom. 1:20, 1 Tim. 1:17, 1 Pet. 5:10, and Deut. 33:27.

Webster's dictionary defines "Eternal" as: having infinite duration; to continue without intermission; perpetual seemingly endless; existing at all times: timeless. Contained within the word "eternal" is the component of Time. Time itself may be understood as the indefinite progression of moments and events continuing forward in apparent irreversible succession. The Bible helps to give us an opportunity to conceive the forward direction simply because the Bible speaks in vivid detail about our future time. We are constantly moving forward in time with hopeful expectation and can somewhat embrace the idea of an eternal future.

Much of eternity past, however, is an enigma to us. As we experience each new moment in forward succession, each moment just experienced becomes eternally past. Each moment of time past is forever fixed as unchangeable, irreversible history. While the events of the past have very real and even valuable effects on our present, as well as our future, only those things we have personally experienced, now kept preserved in our memories, are we able to fully conceive. In reality, most of these past moments called history reach well beyond our very short time of life experience. When dealing with the issue of the beginning of all things, there simply is no other answer except to by Faith trust and believe in the Authority of God's revealed Word, The Bible.

BUT...there are some things we can know about eternity past from the Bible.

The first thing we can know is that God has always existed. God existing in two directions, forward AND backward. Acts 15:18 speaks of eternity past and God's knowing it and all His works in it. Many of us have probably used the word "timeline," which accurately describes what time is from our point of view. The one issue that is difficult to grasp is that the "timeline", in forward progression, is infinite having no apparent end. However, it certainly must have had a beginning. The timeline of earth certainly had a precise beginning and Genesis chapter 1 describes this. Our earth of today also has a predetermined end of its timeline, Matt 24:1-14, Revelation 21:1 explains this truth. It is a unique concept to understand that God created time along with everything else and God alone controls time in all its attributes; past, present, and future. These things are understood best when standing on the firm ground of Faith in what God Himself has revealed in His Word the Bible. This concept is presented in the first chapter and understanding "linear" time as we know it will help process the idea of an Eternally existing God. Faith that God knows what He is doing and trusting Him to do it gives us peace beyond understanding.

The second thing we can know is that God is the Creator of all that exists, and nothing exists outside of His will. The first five words of Genesis 1:1 must be embraced concerning anything that exists, things in Heaven, celestial beings, places and even life itself. Those words, so profound, are this, "In the beginning God Created...".

With this concept we can know and believe that God created everything that exists from His pre-existing position in eternity past. Early in the first chapter of this book we see the celestial beings gathering around the Mountain of God, we must be aware of the central fact that He created the beings, as well as the location where they all exist.

The third thing we can know is that God created celestial beings of different levels of service commonly called Angels. These exist in a dimension that usually cannot be seen by humans. We must understand they are all created beings created by God. There are Cherubim, Seraphim, Archangels, and an entire "Heavenly Host." All have their place and service to Almighty God.

The fourth thing we can know from the Bible is that a leader of these Angels named Lucifer fell from God's favor, covering, and protection because of sin that was found in Him. This is found specifically in Ezekiel 28:12-18. In this passage we also see that Lucifer was the Angel of music. In the translation of the KJV "tabrets and pipes" are mentioned as being created in him. These refer to percussion instruments, and wind instruments. Then we find in Isaiah 14:11-15 that the workmanship of "stringed" instruments was also prepared in him. These three categories of instruments comprise the entire spectrum of musical instruments we now know. This passage also describes the violent expulsion of Satan from Heaven. We can know that he drew a third part of the Angels with him. Revelation 12:9 and following explain this to us.

The fifth thing we can know is that Satan and the fallen Angels reside in darkness. Darkness is their prison and also their chains until the day of judgment. Jude 1:6 tells us this. Their native language is lying and their leader, Satan, is the father of all lies. Darkness, just like light is a place. There is a "place" of light such as a beautiful field on a cloudless day, and there is a place of darkness, such as the depths of a cave. The place of light is a place of warmth, beauty, feeling, peace, and awareness among many other things. The place of darkness is a place of deception, fear, anxiety, harshness, lies, betrayal, and confusion.

We must understand Satan hates God the Father, God the Son, and God the Holy Spirit, he hates Christians, he hates truth, he hates the Jewish nation and everything all these stand for. His goal since his fall from Heaven is to destroy. Revelation 12;1-6 tells of his attempts to destroy Israel from the earth and devour the child born to her.

As you can see, there are many truths we can find in the Bible concerning eternity past, but these still leave a vague representation of what may have been said and how it all came to be.

Certainly, it could have happened as portrayed in this novel approach, the truths of the Bible are in place. This book is simply taking a fictional approach to exploring biblical mysteries and reasonable hypotheses. There is no need to be dogmatic about these things. That approach after all just brings division, and as we will see, that is Satan's main objective.

With all this understood, these truths have been discussed throughout the centuries and every imaginable possibility poured over with scrutiny. This book takes the truths of what is gleaned from the Bible and applies them to what could have been.

Woven into the story, an allegory of truth rises from the pages of what easily could have taken place. The truths we glean from the Word of God causes us to ponder what might have been, but perhaps one important factor in the words written herein is that we may gain a better understanding of the reason for our own spiritual struggles today.

Finally, we may see with better understanding into the war between light and darkness, good and evil and life and death. By understanding better the ultimate power of the Living God, to keep what is His as He protects and provides within a spiritual war zone, we gain a better understanding of the present struggle for the souls of humans.

The Bible clearly illuminates the extreme love God has for His creation, particularly those created in His own image. We can know and embrace His promises to His own. Applying those promises to our lives, we can know that He alone is God and there is none other.

The Beginning

*T*his is the story of the beginning, telling how the Lord God made all the Heavens and the Earth. Before anything was that now exists there was God, the uncaused first cause, complete in all His holy attributes. God the Supreme Being, is unquantifiable and without any limitations. He is real in both substance and personality yet exists not in a particular physical form but as spirit. The effect of God's eternal existence provides for a certain ethereal materialization. This is the glorious composition of God's own being known as His "*Shekinah.*" It is God's "Shekinah Glory" which forms the base DNA of all that is and provides the necessary substrate for anything that exists or ever could exist. It is from this fabric of God Himself that the pattern of all things created will eventually emerge. Having the desire to be creative is just one of His many holy attributes. Creating does not further complete God, it is simply a beautiful outward expression of what is fully contained within His Holy Being. God creates simply for His own good pleasure. God's expressive desire equals the omnipotence of His capabilities as the design in His mind begins to merge with the desires of His heart. Soon God's creative desire will produce works which represent the full content of His glorious design. With the complete image of His plan in mind, the Lord God begins to create every feature of His holy vision. The Shekinah glory of God Himself is like a sea of infinite purity providing the perfect components from which everything finds its genesis. As God's creativity finds full and eternal liberty, His will instantly becomes substance, and every thought and imagination become reality. With each facet of the Master Designer's plan comes a new and more incredible scene that brings to reality every glorious detail of His magnificent imagination.

While the ethereal veil of Shekinah glory slowly begins to rise, the evidence of God's heavenly inspiration is fully revealed. God names this first created place "*Shamayin - Shamayim*" meaning, "Highest Heaven," or "Heaven above the Heavens." It will be the Holiest of all the Holy places. This most beautiful place is located in the center most part of God's being, in the very "heart" of God Himself. It is here atop this pinnacle of creation where God shall establish His Throne of Authority and continue His creative works. Heaven is not only a created place; Heaven will be the center point of all things created hereafter.

With each structure of the Heavenly realm itself now completed, its purposeful intent for habitation is apparent. God continues by creating holy beings who will be the first heavenly inhabitants. God calls these beings Angels. Each Angel is a wonderfully unique individual created and gifted for various intentions and roles. Designations are made evident as God sets in order all the heavenly hosts. Created for the purpose of inhabiting this infinite and incredible new place, they exist in vast quantities serving God and performing particular duties as God's will and plan requires. Angels of the First Order, fantastic living creatures with magnificent features, begin to take their places by standing in closest proximity to the throne at the center of God's own presence. This is the Holiest of all Holy places, the nucleus around which everything is now developing and revolving. Next, second and third orders of Angels begin to manifest. Cherubim, Seraphim, and Archangels all take their places and begin to perform their heavenly appointments.

With the eternal orders now set, all created beings begin to serve in the divine grand design of God's new and perfectly peaceful place called Heaven. The first layer of God's creative works has come to fruition, but soon the fullness of His plan and vision will become a masterpiece of reality.

The peaceful serenity of Heaven's normal atmosphere is suddenly interrupted as the Angel Gabriel is sounding the trumpets of assembly.

Scanning across the vast expanse of the Heavenly landscape, Gabriel's eyes begin to widen as the stunning beauty of God's masterful architecture fills the heavenly horizon. Each feature of the heavenly vista is brilliantly illuminated. Every object is distinctively unique in both design and purpose. All of Heavens structures are set solidly upon massive foundation stones resembling all manners of precious jewels. Flawless in every aspect, each multifaceted stone appears cut with skillful precision and set perfectly in a landscape rich in all precious metals. Every element of Heaven's construction is of such purity that in appearance it is like fine glass and distinguishable only by radiant hues of soft translucent colors. Even the streets glow as pure gold trimmed in fixtures of silver and bronze. Heaven is a place that far exceeds the grandest of imaginations. For one moment, even the Angel Gabriel is captivated with the breathtaking beauty of his surroundings. Quickly, his attention is refocused as the call to assemble continues to echo throughout the heavenly realm. The dazzling beauty of the heavenly landscape is further accented by its inhabitants as multitudes of magnificent Angels are now gathering.

Ebbing and flowing through the heavenly landscape with water-like fluidity, the purity of their beings produces a translucent brilliance of limitless colors, not simply reflections of their environment but light itself emanating from within each heavenly individual. Faster and faster Heaven's inhabitants continue to move as their combining luminescence glows brighter with every passing moment.

With exciting anticipation, like tributaries flowing into one great stream, they rush toward the center point of the heavenly realm known in Heaven's language as "*Har El Elyon.*" Being translated it is, "The Mountain of the Most High God," the Holiest of all Holy places.

Approaching closer to the Holy Mountain of God, more and more details become visible. Proceeding out of the base of the mountain are fountains of pure water, clear as crystal, which immediately divide in all directions forming rivers of living water, cascading throughout the pristine heavenly landscape. Nearer to the base of the Mountain of God the Stones of Fire become visible. Here, six-winged angelic beings called Seraphim can be seen. Seraphim have the unique privilege of remaining closest to their Creator. In reverent response to such close proximity to the Holiness of God, with two of their wings they cover their faces in worshipful adoration; with two wings they cover their feet as an act of humility while standing before God; and with two wings they move swiftly and continually about the Stones of Fire administering the holy response of praise to the Most High God.

Seraphim are continually pouring a clear liquid, which is the Oil of Perfect Praise, from out of golden bowls onto the fiery stones surrounding the Holy Mountain of God. Instantly the liquid is reduced to a mist like vapor which begins to rise upwards, softly gathering to a level just beneath the summit of the lofty Mountain of God. Like burning sweet smelling incense, the aroma fills the space around the Holy Mountain with the most wonderful of fragrances. As the oil of praise is vaporized, the fragrance of the heavenly atmosphere is continually renewed as it spreads throughout all the inhabited realm.

With the uniqueness of the events now unfolding, each of Heavens angelic beings are holding a golden cup filled with the clear oil-like liquid similar to that of the Seraphim. One by one, in rapid succession, the heavenly beings pour out their cups of oil upon the stones of fire. As never before, the fragrance of Heaven is saturated with the most wonderful aroma of praise and worship from all heavenly beings. Located just outside the Stones of Fire is the area of Heaven called the Great Hall where all of the magnificent heavenly Angels are now gathering. As quickly as it began, the movement of assembly was complete.

All of Heavens holy beings are now in perfect position, each one facing intently towards the summit of the Holy Mountain of God. With one accord, in response to the proximity of God's holiness, silence is immediate as they await their next divine directions.

Again, the heavenly trumpets sound as a higher order of created beings begin to appear. They are the Arch Angels of God. Magnificently captivating in their own unique appearance, each one takes their place.

First is Gabriel the Announcer and Messenger of God. Created to herald all heavenly proclamations, he is known to all in Heaven as the Great Communicator. Gabriel takes his place on the first of three elevated platforms. Next to take his place on the second highest platform is Michael the strongest Angel, known throughout Heaven as the Great Protector and Defender of all the heavenly host. Then from a loftier position a created being full of wisdom and perfect in beauty appears. Like a son of the morning, even a bright star shinning in the day, he takes his place upon the highest of the three platforms. The shear brilliance of his countenance outshines any of the other angelic beings assembled. His robe is uniquely woven with every manner of precious stones; diamonds, sapphires, emeralds, and rubies are its coverings. The fringes of his robe are trimmed in pure gold, as clear as crystal. The magnificence of his apparel is like none of the other created beings. Even Michael and Gabriel, both marvelous in their own appearance, are captivated at the splendor of his robe.

At his appearing, all Heaven is immediately filled with every musical sound imaginable. Pulsating with each measure, every resonating tone is individual, distinguishable, and in perfect balance. Every sound of Heaven's melody is being produced as symbiotic faculties radiating outward from this most wonderfully created being. The magnificence of his arms are like eagles wings as they extend outward before the mountain of God. Swiftly they raise towards the audience of the great hall with a commanding presence. Instantly all eyes and attentions are firmly fixed upon this most beautiful one. Perfectly timed in his movements and direction, his voice rings out with a resonating tone that simultaneously brings into harmony all the heavenly beings. From his beginning, leading the heavenly host in worshipful praise is a gifted intention of the Sovereign God who created him. By design he instinctively reacts with perfect interpretation to every action and emotion that proceeds from out of God's Holy Mountain. He is the loveliest of all heavenly beings. He above all others, would find his habitation upon the Mountain of God itself as a Holy Cherub of God. His name is Lucifer, known throughout Heaven as The Anointed Cherub that Covers.

Fulfilling his intended purpose, he begins to score and transpose every action from God into audible sounds. His interpretive response instantly creates an atmosphere of worship that fills Heaven with musical jubilation. Using the most majestic of motions, he begins to direct the assembly and set the tempo note for note in perfect timing. His eyes have a piercing influence and his voice an almost hypnotic vibrato that begins to lift from the assembly a sound of unified worship, praise, and adoration. It was for this purpose he was created.

With increasing anticipation and excitement, the atmosphere of Heaven itself resonates in perfect harmonic response like never before. The actions now proceeding from the Mountain of God are overwhelming, even for an Anointed Cherub. With every passing moment the feeling of great anticipation continues to intensify beyond anything he or any of the beings in Heaven have ever experienced. There is something uniquely special about this event as the Sovereign God is beginning to manifest Himself in visual form. This new experience causes Lucifer himself to sing even more prominently.

With the energy of the moment building, the heavenly population joined in a reveille of praise and worship that produced sounds of such brilliance and wonder that even Lucifer could not contain his emotional response. Like a conductor who is no longer simply directing the symphony but now becoming as one pure embodiment of the musical production itself, Lucifer is captivated by this magnificent sound.

Throughout this refrain, Lucifer leads the focus of the heavenly attention. With every movement there is a response, with every breath from his perfect voice, the heavenly choir follows in harmonic support. He notices how their voices seem to provide accent, adding fullness to his own voice. Continuing to direct this refrain, Lucifer is momentarily distracted by a shimmering reflection just at the edge of his peripheral vision. For the first time he notices his own image as a reflection in the very framework of the heavenly architecture itself. Gazing back at the assembly of heavenly beings, Lucifer draws the obvious conclusion, his beauty and splendor are unmatched in all the heavenly kingdom.

As the apex of the chorus is reached, lightnings flash as the Shekinah Glory of God, in the form of a cloud, begins to engulf the summit of the Holy Mountain. Suddenly, like a whirlwind coming down from the highest regions of the heavenly realm, a great cloud of raging fire churning and infolding upon itself appears. Radiating from out of the midst of the fire is light the color of pure amber, bathing the entire scenery of the heavenly realm in the warmest hues. Proceeding from out of the midst of the brilliant fire, four living creatures appear. Their appearances are like burning coals of fire, like torches moving back and forth and up and down. The noise of their wings is like the noise of great volumes of mighty rushing waters. As the Spirit of God wills, they move. And the movements of the living creatures are as quick as a flash of lightning. When they move, they go straight forward and do not turn to either side. When they stand still, they let down their wings. And this is their appearance; each one has four individual faces, and each one has four wings, and they all sparkle like the color of highly polished brass. Their wings are stretched upward touching at the tips; two wings of every one touching another, and two cover their bodies.

Located above the expanse over their heads is the likeness of a throne, having the appearance of pure precious elements. The throne shimmers as glowing coals with the appearance of fire burning within it. It has brightness round about it like an arch consisting of ribbons of every color imaginable. Suddenly with one swift motion of the Anointed Cherubs wings, silence is immediate. All eyes are immediately covered, and faces bowed down as God Himself, now manifested in a uniquely distinguishable form, proceeds to take His place upon His Throne.

His appearance is like a sudden flash of immeasurable energy having such intensity that for one moment, nothing else in Heaven is visible. For the first time, God is fully revealed and visible to all the heavenly beings. The radiance of His being outshines everything in existence. Clothed with a garment down to the foot and wrapped about the waist is a golden belt. His head and his hairs are white like wool, as white as snow. His eyes were as a flame of fire, and his feet like unto fine brass, as if they burned in a furnace.

The next moments to follow would contain equally unique first-time actions that none of the heavenly beings could have expected. Before now, all things willed by God were impressed directly upon the perfect intellectual nature of each of the heavenly beings without any audible sounds or use of spoken words. With an incredible thundering from out of the midst of the Throne, God begins to speak aloud: *"I Am Alpha and Omega, the Beginning and the End. These things I begin, and all things hereafter shall proceed according as I have foreseen. I Am that I Am. These things I do for a testimony unto all present and all yet to come; All creation shall declare the glory of My Great Love;Through My patience and the works of My Word alone I shall prove My love to all. And of My love there shall be no boundaries, it shall be offered to all unconditionally with unmerited favor. To whosoever will receive My Love, I shall love in full measure. There shall be no separation for those who receive My Love, for I shall establish My loved Ones from everlasting to everlasting. I Am the Alpha and the Omega, the Beginning and the End of all that is and is to come."*

At the power of His voice, all the inhabitants of Heaven exclaimed in unity, "Glory, Glory, Glory to the Righteous Omnipotent God!" Returning to reverent silence, they eagerly await His next action. Revelation upon revelation is the reoccurring theme. Never before has God been visible, never has He spoke with audible voice. With each first-time event brings amazing new experiences for the heavenly population. Within the eternal mind of God, the progression of His grand design has reached a point of convergence. The intention of God's incredible Words have accomplished His purpose, for this is the moment predetermined as "The Genesis Point."

God, in a more unique form, rises up from out of the throne to stand at the right hand of the Majesty on High in preparation for His next incredible action. Once more God speaks aloud: *"Let there be Light."* Immediately as He speaks, the right hand of God begins to open and by the power of His Word alone, the magnificence of a new creation begins.

From out of nothing immediately appears the materialization of all manners of matter itself. Formless and void of organization or identity, this matter comes forth in a brilliant flash, an incredible reaction to God's creative proclamation. Flashing and pulsating with energetic intensity, as if in rhythm with the heavenly heartbeat of God Himself, a new light now emanates from within the palm of His right hand. Those of the great assembly remain awe-stricken in motionless wonder observing as the Word of God continues to create. *"Let this Light be for a distinct separation from the darkness."* With this declaration comes yet another first-time event. As God slowly opens His left hand, those citizens of heavenly origin see the absence of light which God has called "darkness." From their beginning, emanating from within each of the inhabitants of Heaven is the light of life itself. Forever their heavenly expanse has been filled completely with pure light, even the heavenly structures glow in the pristine environment of this Holy realm. They have never experienced the absence of light until now.

Word by Word the creative works of God continue to unfold. *"Let the Light be called Day, And the Darkness shall be called Night."*

Intensely focused upon these new creative actions of God, Lucifer continues to compose with perfect symphonic interpretation of every unfolding event. With effortless precision, Lucifer transposes the visual and breathtaking acts of God by intricately weaving them into the very fabric of the creative melody being produced. There is one new word neither he nor any of the angelic beings have ever heard before, and along with it, a new resonating sound that is the interpretive response to that word. The word which now holds his attention is the new word, "darkness." Lucifer becomes increasingly fascinated by one particular measure of this new melody. As God speaks the word "darkness," the corresponding interpretive response is a low and very powerful impulse that moves like a wave of emotion slowly resonating much longer than any of the other higher tones. None of the other angelic beings seem to give attention to this new tone. Truly he is the more superior being having more enhanced abilities than the others, especially in the area of music. Could it be it is only heard by him? Nevertheless, Lucifer has never experienced anything like this before. He is captivated by its enticingly heavy frequency. His captivation is not limited to only the audible tones of the darkness, but also in its unique appearance. It is simply the absence of all light.

Peering intensely into the darkness, he strains to observe any visible form or shape, but even his superior vision detects nothing. Unwilling to accept the idea of complete nothingness, Lucifer begins to direct more and more of his efforts to pierce this darkness and discover what secret things God must be concealing behind its heavy veil.

Slowly carried away on the wave of this new word, Lucifer finds himself moving farther from the focus of heavenly attention and for the first time, farther away from the Throne of God than ever before.

.Once again God gives a declaration, once again another first-time experience for the heavenly hosts. With the gravity of His Word alone, the unassigned chaos of the new cosmic creation is immediately organized into distinct patterns. Influenced by the grand design conceived within the mind of God Himself, it is the catalyst of His Word which performs the constructive attributes and causes all elemental matter to coalesce. Each particle of matter is codependently bonded at the basic elemental levels. Combining with precision, and modeling His intelligent design, the building blocks of this new cosmic creation are now balanced and in place. Contained within His hands are the power to create all things, and all things are made through Him, and without Him nothing was made that exists. In the strength of His arms, all things are being upheld.

While the ever present Spirit of God hovers attentively over this cosmic "sea" of new beginnings, The Word of God creates the order by which all things hereafter shall transpire. God speaks aloud, "*And the evening and the morning are the First Day.*"

With these words, God has created time itself and set in motion the mechanics and parameters by which this new creation shall operate.

Like unrolling a scroll, the Word of God alone progressively reveals the new creation. These amazing events have completely captivated all angelic attentions, all that is except for one. Lucifer increasingly becomes more involved with his own beautiful appearance and his unique ability to effortlessly provide the score, arrangement, and cadence of God's new creative actions. Never before has there been an event of such magnitude or brilliance that so displayed his own enhanced and obviously superior gifts. By utilizing this new experience of the lower frequency sound wave, he begins building every other interpretive response upon this heavier sounding word now known as darkness.

With such effortless composition, it becomes increasingly obvious that he has no need of any other beings in order to produce his arrangements. He alone contains the "Crescendo" and fullness of all the beautiful heavenly music.

Continuing to build everything upon this frequency of darkness, all other actions and sounds from the creative Word of God slowly begin to grow dim. With each new sensation, Lucifer begins to imagine new opportunities for himself in this new creation. He presumes this must be the intention of the Lord God who created him to be so much higher than all the others. Certainly, God must be creating this new world for him to rule.

With all Angelic attentions focused upon the unique creative events in process, Lucifer is now purposefully moving farther away from the assembly of heavenly beings as he continues to contemplate his own future potential.

As creation continues uninterrupted, God moves as never before. With the progress of the first day's creation stretched out before Him, He sees that it is good. Now reaching down and dipping His hands into the rivers of waters, which flow continually from out of the foot of the throne, God pours out a palm full of the Heavenly water upon the entire framework of creation instantly bringing a certain vitality and a perceptible dimension of depth to all this new work. Moving His hand in a circular motion, God stirs the fluid waters of creation. As He raises His hand from out of the waters, one single droplet clings to the tip of His finger. In form and appearance, it is a beautiful liquid sphere the color of pure sapphire. By the action of His will alone, the single droplet of water is separated from His fingertip and left suspended amid the now slowly revolving sea of creation. It came from the waters, and it is in the waters, yet it is kept somehow distinctively separate from the vast waters surrounding it.

Now focusing intensely upon this single sphere, The Word of God is heard: "*Let there be a Heaven and Earth. Let there be an expanse, a firmament in the midst of the waters, and let it divide the Waters.*" And God made the firmament to divide the waters above from the waters below, and it was so. And God called the firmament, "*Shemim*" to mean expanse above, or Sky.

And the evening and the morning were the second day.

Again, the Word of God speaks: "*Let the waters under the sky be gathered together into one place, and let the dry land appear*"; and immediately it was so. And God called the dry land Earth, and the gathering together of the waters He called Seas.

And God saw that it was good.

Then again He said, "*Let the earth bring forth grass, the herb that yields seed, and the fruit tree that yields fruit according to its kind, whose seed is in itself, on the earth*"; and it was so. And immediately the earth began to grow all manners of vegetation and grasses, the herb that yields seed according to its kind, and the tree that yields fruit, whose seed is in itself according to its kind. And God saw that it was good.

And the evening and the morning were the third day.

The Fall

*A*s God's creation continues, self-indulgence is becoming an engulfing obsession for Lucifer. More and more distracted from the creative actions of God, Lucifer is slowly being carried further away by his self-absorbed intrigue. No longer noticing the completion of another incredible moment in the new creative actions of the Almighty, Lucifer continues to focus more and more on himself.

The beautiful musical accompaniment that once so purely reflected every creative action of God is slowly being replaced by a darker, much heavier cadence. Every thought and emotional experience of Lucifer is now being incorporated into the musical melody being produced. With each passing moment, original created natures and characteristics begin to decompose as loyalty turns to pride, service is replaced by self-centered ego, love and reverence degrade into arrogance and conceit.

Becoming completely engulfed by his own conceited imaginations and illusions of grandeur, Lucifer finds himself far away from any other created being. Fully lost in his pride-filled aspirations and newly found indulgences, he contemplates his fantasy. This new creation is the perfect opportunity. A new kingdom deserves a new king, a ruler with new powers, new ways. Suddenly, unable to contain as mere thought any longer, he speaks aloud, "A new creation deserves a new god!"

Lucifer, becoming increasingly more obsessed with this fantastic possibility, exclaims again, "And what god is without subjects who will bow before him and worship him!" Casting his gaze towards the masses of unsuspecting heavenly beings, he sees his opportunity.

Lucifer, originally created by God as the Anointed Cherub and once seen in appearance as the brightest among the inhabitants of Heaven, is now far from being a bright morning star. All Godly characteristics are now anti-God in nature; love turns into hate, and praise becomes pride. To be worshipped like God has now become his singular and central desire. This once pure "Anointed Cherub" has now become the very seed of unholy desires.

Surrounding him like a turbulent rage of cyclonic emotion, Lucifer embraces the darkness. The sphere of blackness now surrounding Lucifer is the result of every evil intention found within his newly fallen nature. His original pure and peaceful character has irreversibly become an adversarial arrogance. Blinded so completely by this self-conceived cloud of deception, everything else around him is of no concern, even the awesome and ongoing creative actions of God have gone unnoticed.

Lucifer's self-centered focus is startled back to the reality of the moment as the voice of God rings out once again confirming the completion of yet another incredible creative action.

And the evening and the morning were the fourth day.

Like a dark sphere, this wicked lust for power and the desire to be worshipped is now surrounding Lucifer. Slowly he turns and begins advancing towards the great assembly of Angels. With a focused intensity he silently watches from within this new cloak of darkness. Undetected, he continues moving slowly around the perimeter of the assembly. Silently he observes, like a predator stalking his prey, carefully seeking which will be the first of the heavenly beings to be approached.

So completely captivated are the angelic beings by the creative actions of God, this inconceivable evil now approaching remains completely unnoticed. Fully veiled in darkness, Lucifer's hypnotic rhythm of deception advances toward the crowd of angelic beings. Using whispering tones of enticement, he slowly moves, patiently circling the assembly of Angels. Eventually, there is movement by one individual in the outermost edge of the assembly. The focus of the first Angel has been broken. The attention that was once so completely focused on God's creative actions has now turned toward the dark sphere silently approaching.

The time has come, Lucifer's first victim has been selected. With an innocent curiosity, the Angel moves toward the sphere unaware that the first gaze into pure darkness could be its last. Feeling a strange magnetism, the Angel becomes fixated upon this unique object. Everything that the heavenly being has ever seen or known until now has been bathed in the purity of God's light. The attraction of the sphere is found in its unique appearance. It is the absolute absence of all light.

Moving closer to this sphere, a strange feeling of excitement begins to develop within the Angel. Upon closer inspection, the Angel's excitement quickly turns to caution. With suspicions aroused, the Angel hesitates. Immediately from within the black sphere comes a strangely familiar voice, a voice of intrigue, enticing the Angel to move closer to the darkness. Inching ever closer to the object, the Angel narrows its vision to see a shadow like form beginning to become visible. It has a vaguely familiar resemblance of the Anointed One known as Lucifer. Speaking calmly in quiet tones, as not to attract attention, Lucifer continues to encourage the Angel to move closer. "Do not fear, I have brought to you a great opportunity to join with me in this wonderful new creation of God. God needs guardians to rule over this new realm of creation." The Angel quickly responds, "I have heard of no such offer from God." Lucifer replies, "That is why I'm here. I am to present this only to those who I find worthy of the position."

Sensing the hesitancy of the Angel, Lucifer continues, "If it is the appearance of the darkness that offends you, remember that it was

God Himself that made the separation between the light and this darkness. This darkness you see is merely the gateway into this new realm of God's creation." Lucifer speaks with more persistence, "Just start with a touch, then you will see that there is nothing to fear."

Lucifer continues in his deceptive distraction, "Look at me, I am embracing the darkness and I have not been harmed. What harm can come from a simple touch?" Contemplating the situation, curiosity is stronger than caution and the Angel yields to the attraction. With one glance back at the light of the creative events still unfolding, the Angel turns and reaches out to make contact with the strange anomaly. Driven by curious desire, the heavenly being has past the point of no return. Upon contact with the sphere's outer horizon, all light from its heavenly life is instantly absorbed and swallowed up. A being who just moments before was filled so brilliantly with pure light, is now reduced to a hollow shell void of light. Blinded by the darkness, there is no hope of ever escaping the vacuum like clutches of this void.

The first casualty of Lucifer's deceitful plan has fallen. Lucifer's first conquest is the beginning of a chain reaction. Holy Beings, disturbed by the presence of the sphere, turn to look. One by one they make their choice, one by one those who chose to move away from God are reduced from beings of light, into hopeless prisoners of darkness. Beings once so brilliantly beaming with pure light are now void of all light and the life it brings.

With each conversion, Lucifer gains more and more confidence. Moving across the vast assembly of angelic beings, Lucifer's sphere of deceit continues to grow, enlarging itself with each fallen Angel.

While Heaven's attention is still focused upon the works of creation, Lucifer seizes the opportunity to continue his deceptive harvest. Holy Angels, never intending to turn their backs on God, find the power of this dramatic new medium so persuasive that once they look into this abyss and begin to listen to the rhythmic tones of darkness, their ability to see or hear anything else vanishes.

Blinded by the absence of light, each fallen Angel can now only follow the familiar voice that is emanating from out of the center of this dark sphere of deception. Each victory only fans the flame of pride that has now completely consumed the heart of the once pure Anointed Cherub that Covers.

One by one, Angels are turned from God. One by one, their pure light and heavenly vision fades forever into the abyss of Lucifer's inescapable singularity of darkness.

Meanwhile Creation continues as The Word of God rings aloud, *"Let the waters bring forth abundantly the moving creature that has life, and fowl that may fly above the earth in the open firmament of Heaven."* And God created great whales, and every living creature that moves, which the waters brought forth abundantly, after their kind, and every winged fowl after his kind: and God saw that it was good.

And God blessed them, saying, *"Be fruitful, and multiply, and fill the waters in the seas and let fowl multiply in the earth."*

And the evening and the morning were the fifth day.

Lucifer's army of fallen Angels is growing exponentially with each conversion, engulfing all who will choose the darkness rather than the light. Pressing inward layer by layer, his cloud of deception grows with every passing moment. With each whisper of his enticing words, Lucifer is bringing certain destruction to the pristine environment of God's heavenly realm.

Conversions continue at an alarming rate while God, by His Word alone, continues His creation.

With increasing ferocity, Lucifer's dark sphere of deception moves around the outer fringes of angelic hosts like a prowling lion, devouring any in the crowd who will choose to turn away from God. One brief moment of consideration is all that is needed, just a glance into the face of darkness and their temptation soon becomes their eternal torment.

With his rapidly increasing army of darkness, Lucifer's advance continues skimming through the outer ranks of the angelic beings gathered around the Throne of God. Perceiving God to be completely preoccupied with His new creations, Lucifer continues in his mutinous rebellion. Lucifer has now drawn almost one-third of the entire assembly of angelic beings from God's pure light into his consuming and blinding darkness.

However, not every Angel has succumbed to the rapidly increasing gravity of his influence. Holy Angels who refused the temptation of Lucifer to turn away from God are pressing inward, converging ever closer toward the Mountain of God which is now the singular source of light and the only hope for their protection.

Unified in choice, their fusion of faithfulness produces a luminosity which rapidly increases to orders of magnitude never before experienced in all of Heaven. In response to their faithful choice, God provides protection against the temptations of Lucifer's invading darkness. In one brilliant eruption of omnipotent energy, God produces a tremendous dome of pure light emanating from out of the base of the Throne of God located high above the Holy Mountain. Completely encircled by this dome of protection, all of the heavenly realm, including His new cosmos of creation, is sealed and safe.

Stunned and temporarily blinded by the sudden flash of energetic light, the progression of Lucifer's deceitful influence comes to an abrupt halt. Sustained by God's own power, the illumination of pure energy and light has removed Lucifer's cloak of darkness revealing all those who have now fallen.

The dome of protection is completely restricting the ability of Lucifer and his fallen army of darkness to approach any closer. Lucifer himself is left completely disoriented. Groping about helplessly he shouts, "What just happened!"

As his sight begins to return, Lucifer is unable to see through this new incredible barrier that is stopping his progress. Feverishly Lucifer circles, again and again searching for an area of weakness where he can refocus his attack. Frustrated by the impenetrable dome of light now surrounding all things created, Lucifer exclaims once more, "What is happening, I cannot see anything inside this barrier!" With this one sovereign action God has sealed forever the fate of all heavenly beings according to their choice. To those who chose to remain in the light, they shall forever be kept in the light and given the power to overcome the darkness. To those who have chosen darkness, they shall forever be lost, irreversibly condemned to an eternity of absolute darkness without hope or possibility of recovery.

Inside the protected space of the dome of light, God continues with His work of new creation. God again speaks aloud, but this time is different. God has always spoken in first person singular when creating or otherwise commanding. Once again, a unique event happens as God appears to speak in plurality, as if speaking with Himself, *"Let Us make man in Our own Image."*

At these words a most remarkable thing happens next. God, still ever present in Heaven, begins to manifest Himself in a physical form onto the newly created Earth. His countenance is far brighter than the sun shining at full strength. His head and hair are white like wool of the most perfect lamb, white as pure snow. His eyes are like the flames of a fire and His two feet are like highly polished brass as if refined in a furnace.

Now standing upright upon the newly created earth, the Lord God looks to the ground and sees His own image outlined in the form of His shadow. Using His own hands, He begins a new and unique work. Taking great care and with intricate precision, the Lord God creates from the dust of the ground a most wonderfully unique form patterned after His own image and likeness. Kneeling beside the newly formed figure, the Lord God looks intensely up into the third Heaven. With eyes fixed upon the Throne, the Lord God begins to inhale deeply. From out of the midst of the Throne of God a very distinctive presence is transferred into the nostrils of the Lord God. Then slowly the Lord God exhales, breathing directly into the nostrils of the figure He has formed from the dust of the ground. Filled with the breath of life, immediately man became a unique living being having an eternally living soul.

Taking him by the hand, the Lord God lifts the man to his feet. With a voice as the sound of mighty waters the Lord God exclaims, *"This is man made in Our image, according to Our likeness; to him is given dominion over all living creatures upon the whole earth."* So the Lord God made man in His own image and likeness and named him Adam.

With great joy the Lord God plants a special garden in this highly favored place He calls "Eden", and there He put the man whom He had formed to tend and keep it. And out of the ground the Lord God made every tree grow that is pleasant to the sight and good for food.

Standing in the middle of the garden, in the precise place where God formed man from the ground, God placed a very special tree called "The Tree of Life". Located nearby was another unique tree, "The Tree of the Knowledge of Good and Evil." Speaking directly to Adam, the Lord God said, "*I have given you every herb that yields seed which is on the face of all the earth, every tree whose fruit produces seed; to you it shall be for food.*" Focusing Adam's attention, the Lord God continues speaking. "*Of every tree of the garden you may freely eat; but of the tree of the knowledge of good and evil you shall not eat, for in the day that you eat of it you shall surely die.*"

From out of the ground the Lord God formed every beast of the field and every bird of the air. God speaks aloud to Adam, "*To every beast of the earth and every bird of the air, I have given every green herb for their food.*" And so it was, that all living creatures would eat of the fruits and herbs of the land. From every animal of the field and of all the birds that fly that the Lord God has created, He brings two of each kind, a male and a female, before the man Adam to see what he would call them. And whatever Adam calls each one, that becomes it's name.

The Lord God, wanting Adam to understand that he is created different from all the other creatures, shows him compatible couples from each kind, one male and one female of the same kind. But of all the kinds of creatures, there is not found any comparable companion suitable for Adam. Knowing the uniqueness of Adam, the Lord God does not wish him to be the only one of his kind, so the Lord God decides to make for Adam a comparable companion.

For Adam to be fruitful and multiply, he needs a partner of similar kind having his own unique nature and design. So the Lord God causes a deep sleep to come upon the man Adam whereafter He removed a rib bone from Adam's side. The Lord God closed the wound perfectly, leaving no marks or scarring. Taking the rib of the man, the Lord God carefully forms with intricate precision a new body similar in appearance to Adam, differing only in features. The Lord God calls this new creation Woman, and as with Adam He also breathes life and spirit into her.

Having shown to the first man the sacred order of procreation, one male and one female of the same kind, the woman God created is the perfect comparable companion suitable for the man Adam, and Adam is the perfect comparable companion suitable for the woman.

Then God sees everything that He had made, and indeed it is very good. So, the evening and the morning are the sixth day. Now the Heavens and the earth, and all the host of them, are finished. And on the seventh day, God ends all His work. Then God blesses the seventh day and sanctified it, because in it He rested from all His creative works.

So it was that both the man and the woman walked together this sanctified seventh day in perfect fellowship in this pristine utopian garden of God called Eden.

Together the Man and the Woman enjoy their first day in Eden as the Lord God Himself walks with them throughout all the land.

The stunning beauty of this world is overshadowed only by the present and perfect Holiness of God Himself. Being created in God's own image and likeness, the Man and Woman also appear as rare and precious jewels in this most perfect environmental setting.

Seeing that the Man and the Woman are perfectly matched, the Lord God's heart is filled with joy. God stops moving and takes the Man whom He has made in His right hand and the woman whom He has made in His left hand and presents woman to man and man to woman. Upon taking hold of the woman's hand, Adam declares "This is flesh of my flesh, bone of my bone!" The Lord God, clasping both of their hands tenderly in His proclaims, *"What I have joined together, let no one separate."* Looking at the man He speaks, *"You shall be a husband, to this woman, You shall love her and cherish her as your own flesh,"* and turning to the woman He says, *"You shall be a wife to this man. You shall love him and cherish him as your own flesh."* And they were both naked, the man and his wife, but were not ashamed for the purity of their innocence was surrounding each of them like a shining robe of light.

Adam, still gazing into the beautiful eyes of his wife, exclaims once more, loudly for all of creation to hear, "This is my wife, and she will be called Eve for she is first among women!"

All creatures hear the jubilant proclamation from their guardian governor as Adam's announcement of Eve echoes throughout the new earth. The wind itself heralds the jubilant news of Adam's decree, causing all creatures great and small to react with a joyful excitement. The great oceans seemingly respond with crashing waves in reaction to Adam's joyous announcement. All of the new earth appears to celebrate and rejoice.

As Adam and his wife Eve seal their Holy union with a tender kiss and embrace, the Lord God pronounces His blessings, *"Be fruitful and multiply. Fill the earth and govern it for I will cause it to yield in abundance to you."*

With this one proclamation comes only one warning, The Lord God has given to Adam only one law they are to obey, *"Of every tree of the garden you may freely eat; but of the tree of the knowledge of good and evil you shall not eat, for in the day that you eat of it you shall surely die."* Now joined hand in hand, the two "newlyweds" continue walking together as one. United in mind and spirit, both are enjoying more fully the splendors of this edenic paradise.

The Lord God turns and begins ascending into the sky back into the third Heaven, all the while observing the two beings He loves most in this vast new creation.

Meanwhile, outside the protected space of the dome of light, Lucifer is growing increasingly frustrated as he slowly begins to realize what has happened. God was not distracted nor unaware of events transpiring outside His new creation as Lucifer had originally perceived. It was God Himself who produced this impenetrable barrier. To those now left outside the dome, the surface appears reflective like a mirror. For the first time since his choice to rebel against

God, Lucifer sees his own reflection and his current state of being. His once pure and unmatched beauty is now void of any favorable or appealing features. Now, only a dark and lifeless image of by gone splendor, his reflection is merely a shadow of the magnificent being he once was.

Lucifer's own mutinous actions have culminated in one irreversible direction having only one outcome. The inevitable war for the control of this new creation has begun. In uncontrolled arrogance and pride, Lucifer exclaims to his army of darkness, "This is of no consequence, I will soon control all of this new world as well as all of Heaven!" Realizing he has multiplied legions of Angels under his sinister control, Lucifer gazes upward to see God now seated upon His throne high above the dome of protection. Arrogantly Lucifer exclaims again, "I will continue my assault upon the Throne of the Most High!" Belligerently, his outburst of insulting insinuations continues. He gives directions to his newly swayed masses as they begin to advance towards the Mountain of God's Throne. At that moment, Almighty God swiftly focuses His attention. With eyes now burning like flames of fire, God fixes His gaze upon the leader of the advancing army of darkness. All the heavenly beings kept safely inside the protection of the dome bow immediately in reverent silence.

Drunkenly caught up in his own vision of grandeur, Lucifer continues his rantings to boast and brag, speaking vile obscenities as he commands his influenced followers forward. Lucifer, now fully lost in his own lusts, continues in his vocal exclamations. "I will ascend above the height of the Holy Mountain of God, and I will sit upon the throne!" His true nature now culminates in one raging moment of insanity and insatiable arrogance as Lucifer faces the Almighty God and screams in tones of blasphemy and defilement, "I WILL BE GOD AND ALL BEINGS SHALL WORSHIP ME!" In that very instant, with all righteous power and glory, God stands and speaks, "*Silence!*"

At these words, the dome of protection progressively becomes transparent as the Mountain of God and all the heavenly hosts of the great assembly, slowly become visible to those beings kept outside the dome in the darkness. Immediately, Lucifer is silenced and his army of fallen Angels are instantly immobilized by God's command.

Suspended helplessly in the outer darkness surrounding the dome of protection, Lucifer and those fallen ones with him can only listen as God begins to speak, "*You My Anointed Cherub who covers; remember, it was I who established you. I created you with all beauty and splendor above all the other beings. I placed you highest above all the angelic hosts, you only were permitted on My Holy Mountain. You above the others, were permitted to walk back and forth in the midst of the fiery stones. Now, because of your beauty, your heart is swollen; You have corrupted your wisdom for the sake of your own splendor; You have made filthy that which was once righteous. Oh how you have fallen My Anointed Cherub! You have defiled your sanctuaries by the multitude of your sins and by the obscenity of your deeds. Therefore, let it be known; By your own choice, the revelation of 'Darkness' has brought fire from your midst, but through your own pride it has completely devoured you! No longer shall you be known as Lucifer, The*

Anointed Cherub that Covered. Now from this day and forevermore you shall be called Satan, for you alone are My Adversary. By your own choice, you have conceived evil in your heart, and it has consumed you fully. You, Satan, are hereby stripped of all righteous privileges; your once perfect voice will be like a hissing voice full of guile and deceit before me. You are also a Devil and a liar, and the truth shall no longer be found within you; For you have become the father of all lies! A God you shall never be, but a Prince and ruler of darkness you have fully become. It is war against Me that you seek, so then war you shall have!

With every word that proceeds from God, the dome of light continues to expand in all directions pushing Satan and his fallen Angels further and further away from the protected pristine environment of the Heavenly realm.

Again, God speaks to Satan with a thunderous voice:*"From this moment forward your actions shall only produce failures, your words shall be lies and your wisdom shall be forever as foolishness before me. My pure nature and love shall be made manifest, for wherever you cause sin to prosper, My Grace shall prosper far more!"* Widening His gaze to include the immense cloud of fallen Angels, God continues His Judgement decree: *"And to those Angels who by choice have fallen from their first estate, those who preferred darkness over light, they shall be your subjects, your demons, held by your chains of darkness and controlled by your unrighteous indignation until the fullness of days. They shall be kept in darkness, reprobate minds without any hope of recovery and reserved for everlasting punishment at My final judgement of all the wicked! From the beginning, I have seen all things, both*

35

good and evil. All things which shall hereafter come to pass, on earth and in Heaven are according to My will and only by My permission! This is My Word, it is forever established, and it is forever settled!"

Rising to his feet, Michael the great Archangel of God, is the first to raise his voice in resolute acknowledgement of God's sovereign commandment, "As God has spoken, so let it be written in Heaven, so let it be done in all creation!" With this proclamation, all the Holy Angelic Hosts raised themselves in allegiance to the Mighty God and exclaimed in unity, "Holy, Holy, Holy! Worthy to be praised, the one and only God who was and is and is to come!"

Rising from out of the assemble of holy Angels is the Prince and leader of the heavenly armies. Now the highest among those ranked in Heaven, Michael gives the command to Heaven's host, "Take up the armor of God and dress fully that you may be able to withstand the evil of this day!" Immediately, the armies of Holy Angels are arrayed in the full armor of God's protective righteousness.

Peering through the transparent dome, Michael fixes his eyes upon the leader of the fallen ones, now known forever as Satan the Devil. As the two opponents stare eagerly into each other's eyes, unspoken memories of past splendor and unity are but a fleeting reminder of their original estate, and of a time now forever lost.

As their eyes narrow in complete adversarial anger, God stands from His seat of righteous judgement and gives the command from which there is no opportunity for arbitration, *"I Am Alpha and*

Omega, the Beginning and the End. There is No Other God besides Me! Depart immediately from Me and My heavenly abode all you workers of iniquity!" With those final words, the dome of protection is suddenly removed.

Michael, raising his sword in allegiance to the Throne of God, rushes swiftly forward leading the great armies of Heaven against the multitudes of fallen ones under Satan's command.

And war breaks out in Heaven as Michael and his righteous Angels fight against Satan who is the Devil, and his fallen Angels. Though Satan and his armies fight hard against Michael and the heavenly hosts they do not prevail, for Heaven's army is far stronger than Satan's.

Quickly pressed hard into submission by the mighty armies of God, Satan, now surrounded by his helpless legions of demons, is found cowering in humiliating defeat.

Michael, that great prince of God, raises his sword in victory as he takes hold of Satan by the neck and lifts him to eye level. Writhing like a captured serpent, Satan cannot break the grip of Michael's strong hand. Pausing only momentarily, Michael looks deeply into the darkened eyes of his once fellow servant of God. Now with full realization and understanding that all goodness and hope was truly gone, Michael, with all of his might, violently hurls him out of the heavenly realm.

Like a great burning comet spiraling downward and having for a tail the great cloud of fallen Angels, Satan passes through the second level of the Heavens called the cosmos, the space containing all the newly created celestial bodies.

So that great deceiver called the Devil and Satan is cast down from God's heavenly dwelling place, and all his Angels with him. They are defeated, and neither is a place found for them in God's Heaven any longer.

The war in Heaven has ended in complete victory for all its Holy inhabitants. Eternally secure, peace and serenity are once again restored to the Heavenly Kingdom.

With great velocity, Satan continues to tumble uncontrollably through the vast universe of God's new creation until finally entering the atmosphere surrounding the pristine new creation called Earth.

With the battle for Heavenly control forever settled, the war between good and evil has only begun. Satan's destructive deception will soon find roots for a new beginning.

The Deception

eyond the vast blackness of the cosmos, God's dome of protection fully encapsulates the entire heavenly habitation.

Once again, the dome is no longer transparent but appears indistinguishable from the surrounding cosmos of creation. God and all of the heavenly realm are no longer visible to those who were banished outside the barrier of the protective dome.

With a resounding heavenly momentum, Satan's impact upon this pristine and beautiful new world called Earth is made evident. So forceful is the impact that the ground erupts with a violent upheaval of water instantly turned to vapor as soil and stone are also crystalized. An area once covered with lush green forests, teaming with life, has now been reduced to a barren, desolate wasteland.

Located far away in Eden's Garden, Adam and his wife Eve are so wonderfully entranced in developing their new relationship, they continually exclaim loudly their joyful experiences. The two are unaware of the arrival of pure evil that has made the first unholy marks upon their perfect new world.

In the far reaches of the earth, the whispering of the winds has reached the ears of the one who just arrived, an intruder who is not originally of this world, but is now the outcast enemy of God.

In this world of purity and light, the evidence of Satan's fall is made clear by his dark visual appearance. His robe once brilliant and pure, now appears permanently blackened and scorched by the friction of falling with such forceful velocity through earth's thick atmosphere. His countenance also appears despairingly destitute, for it too has fallen from a great and lofty height.

As the dust begins to settle, Satan rises from out of the impact crater and stares in frustration at the Heavens searching to see the realm of God's habitation. The totality of his rage and the unbridled hatred contained within him is like a great deluge, washing away the ability to experience any good emotion. His thoughts and intentions are permanently and continually evil. Revenge is the only comprehensible feeling he has left. Forever blinded by his own pride and fueled by his unbridled hatred of God, Satan looks up into the Heavens and narrows his black, lifeless eyes as the judgement of God continues to ring loudly in his reprobate mind. With vile and belligerent speech, he vows that his opposition of God will last forever.

Completely engulfed in his rage, Satan plots his revenge, "God Himself must be impacted at His most vulnerable estate, my retaliation will be without mercy!" Satan, a supernatural being, has abilities that far exceed any found in this realm. Leaping upward into the sky, he swiftly begins circling higher and higher above the surface of the earth. Lurking in the atmosphere above the earth, Satan begins scanning the planet looking for any opportunity to begin his attack. Methodically he circles the globe, frustratingly moving back and forth, up and down again and again.

While traveling eastward, a brilliant illumination catches his black, sinister eyes. As a shining star set apart from its surroundings, Adam and Eve appear as points of light unique in all creation. Satan identifies his point of interest and begins to observe the intimate fellowship between Adam and Eve. These most unusual creatures have a familiar image and likeness Satan can only compare to the likeness of God Himself. Hating even the very image of God, Satan formulates a plan. "These special beings are obviously highly favored above all of creation since they are fashioned in the very image of God Himself." Therefore, he supposes, "Tormenting and corrupting them would be like a stabbing pain in the very heart of God." It is at that moment Satan realizes in order for this scheme to work, the relationship between these first two beings and God Himself must somehow be broken.

As his previous experience in Heaven has proven, it is much easier to deceive one individual at a time. He will use the same tactical approach here, divide the two, separate them from each other, and most importantly, entice one to turn away from the presence and power of God Himself.

Satan, identifiably not of this new world, searches for a disguise, anything to mask his true identity. As he looks diligently, he sees a potential candidate. It is a Leviathan, the most impressive of all the creatures in the new world. Massive in size and strength yet very skillful in its movements, Leviathan's formidable features are accented by a unique and wonderfully captivating appearance. Leviathan has the ability to change the color of its skin, making it almost indistinguishable with the surroundings. Satan quietly follows the creature, observing and even mimicking it's every movement.

Slowly approaching the creature, Satan ponders, "What could be your name?" The creature pauses and looks at Satan with a calm and brief curiosity, then continues moving in a lumbering yet graceful fashion. Satan, finding this creature to be captivating, is satisfied this is the disguise he needs.

Increasingly unsettled by the constant shadowing of Satan, the creature turns once more and looks inquisitively as if to ask this newly found shadow, "What is it that you seek of me?" Satan whispers, "I'm sure the name that simple creature Adam gave you is not very 'creative' so let me give you one that is as grand as you are." Pausing for just a moment, Satan speaks, "I shall call you "Zikeet-Nahash." Realizing that camouflage is a very unique ability, Satan continues speaking, "Because your true identity can be hidden, you will prove to be very useful to me."

More and more the giant becomes less sensitive to the constant exposure and whispering voice of this persistent follower. Finally reaching a particular destination, the creature stops and lowers its massive head. Now looking into the face of Satan, with inquisitive eyes, the creature's curiosity seems obvious. Surprised at the creature's alert intuitiveness, Satan speaks aloud, "I have a rather simple request, I seek a dwelling place, a 'habitation,' so to speak." Continuing to speak softly, Satan begins to extend his hand to the giant he now refers to as "Zikeet-Nahash." Satan exclaims, "I am alone, an outcast with no place or association." Leviathan responds with an action of compassion (which is the original nature of all the creatures on the new earth), as he places his head under the extended hand of Satan.

A single gesture of friendship is silently offered, an innocent invitation to continue along together becomes an unspoken communication which Satan easily understands. Moving in closer with a sinister expression and a soft evil laughter, Satan replies, "I have something else in mind, an agreement of sort." The creature lowers its massive head as Satan whispers softly in the giant's ear, "Actually more like a union, but with some major changes!" The creature, now referred to as Zikeet-Nahash, as if agreeing to the proposal of Satan, lowers its massive body in a gesturing offer of subtle submission. Immediately Satan takes hold of the giant creature's head. In that one moment, Satan, the master of deceit, is now in control of the impressive creature's mind and body. The subtle gestures of this yielding creature will soon play to Satan's sinister advantage.

Continuing their exploration, Adam and Eve reach a unique place in this paradise of Eden. There is so much life and beauty everywhere, the two stop for a moment in awe of the beautiful garden that God had planted especially for them. Captivated by the perfection of this place, they both feel a deep connection with every aspect of the environment. With each beat of their heart, the beauty and perfect peace of Eden fill their beings with complete joy, so complete and full it is beyond expression.

There is a large river coming from out of Eden, which flows eastward to water the garden which the Lord God had planted, and from there it parts into four crystal clear streams. While Adam continues on past where the river forks, Eve continues walking along the shoreline, meandering without concern, as the fragrances in reaction to her presence fill the air with the most wonderful scents. The abundance of life is overwhelming. The rivers are teeming with all manners of fish and aquatic life. Each kind gathers in response to Eve's presence as if drawn to her by some sense of fascination. So peaceful and accepting are all the creatures that Eve cannot help but wonder, if she were to speak to them, could any of them speak back to her?

Intrigued by this possibility, Eve begins to speak to every living thing she encounters. They certainly respond to her voice and actions, and she somehow seems to intuitively interpret their responses. It is not with words as she and Adam could communicate, it is different. It is an unspoken understanding, like a common connection between her and all earth's creatures. Continuing her walk, she repeatedly speaks to animals of all types, both large and small.

All responded with audible sounds and vocalizations, but none are able to speak in the language she and Adam use.

Structured vocal communication that conveys both emotion and thought is apparently a unique ability only she, Adam, and the Lord God Himself possess.

While walking along the banks of the river, she has grown very fond of one of the smaller animals that she recalls Adam naming, Cat. It is a very calming, and soothing creature with a unique sound, a humming, purring sound that Eve finds very soothing. As Eve sits down, the cat seems to invite her to hold it and even embrace it. The cat seems to enjoy the gentile strokes of Eve as she caresses the animal's soft fur with her hand.

So engulfed in her exploration of this fascinating new world, Eve does not notice how far away she is from her husband Adam. This is the first time she has been alone since her creation. With the cat now peacefully sleeping in her arms, Eve turns back, retracing the shoreline of the river. While walking along the shoreline, she ponders, "Maybe Adam can speak to the other creatures, after all he gave them their names." She reasons, "Certainly he would know if there were any that can speak to us." In hopeful anticipation, she continues to follow the river back towards the place she was last together with Adam.

Lurking deep in the shadows of the lush Edenic vegetation, there is one unseen observer who has been silently following Eve. This creature is not like any of the other creatures. This creature is no longer what it appears to be. Now more cunning than any beast of the field which the Lord God had made, it is the only creature in all of creation which has the ability to camouflage its body and drastically alter its appearance. The face of the creature is pleasant, somewhat resembling the faces of Adam and Eve, in fact it is quite beautiful in appearance, however that is where the resemblance stops. It's body is more elongated and covered with a skin that is made up of a double coat of scale-like facets that appear to reflect it's surroundings with every exposure to light. His back is made of rows of shields, impenetrably seamed together. This creature, having four legs, prefers to move in a horizontal posture rather than a vertical one like the humans. It is the most unique creature found in all of Eden.

With Leviathan now submissively under his control, Satan moves into action. This is the opportunity Satan has been waiting for.

As Eve continues walking alone, a voice from within the creature speaks out softly to Eve saying, "Hello." Eve stops and quickly turns around. Somewhat startled by this voice, she looks intensely up and down the shoreline speaking back in hopeful response, "Hello, who is it that speaks to me?" After several attempts with no other response, Eve is disappointed and convinced that it is possibly the sounds of the river as it ebbs and flows, or maybe the breeze rustling through the trees. As Eve turned again to leave, the voice unmistakably resonates again. "Hello Eve, wife of Adam, cherished above all of God's creations." Suddenly the cat who had become Eve's companion along the way leaps from her arms and quickly disappears into the forest.

Eve turns to see a creature barely visible, with only its face distinguishable among the thick vegetation and the trees of the lush Edenic forest. Again, the creature speaks, "Do not fear, I mean no harm." Eve, having no prior experience of fear, speaks back, "I am not afraid, I am only intrigued by your ability to speak to me. Come out where I can see you fully and tell me your name?" The creature replies, "You may call me Zikeet, for what you see is not all that I am." Again, Eve requests, "Come out into the light where I may see all of you." Zikeet replies, "Not yet at least not here." Eve laughingly comments, "You are a shy one! Tell me Zikeet, are there others who can speak with me as you do?" Zikeet replies, "No, all the others are non-speaking creatures, inferior to those of us who can speak the language of a God." He continues, "In fact, this world was created so we three could rule and have dominion over it all. Even the fruit of the trees are for us to enjoy." Looking at Eve he asks, "Have you tasted all of the fruit of the garden?" Eve replies, "I have not yet tasted all of the fruits of the garden." Zikeet continues, "Has God not said, 'You should eat of every tree?" And Eve says to Zikeet, "Indeed, we may eat the fruit of the trees of the garden." Lifting her hand, she points towards the center of the garden area. "But of the fruit of a particular tree, the tree which is in the very middle of the garden He has said, 'You shall not eat it, nor shall you touch it, lest you die.' "

Eve unknowingly has just revealed privileged information to an unknown agent with evil intentions. Satan, though a superior being to any found on the earth, is not omniscient, neither is he omnipresent. He does, however, have a far superior mind and enhanced abilities of intuition that combine to give him distinct intellectual advantages over any other created being on this earth. Zikeet probes further with another question. "What is this forbidden Tree called?" Eve again provides the answer that completes the plan for Satan's wicked scheme. "It is called the Tree of Knowledge of Good and Evil," she replies.

Satan, created highest of all the angelic beings, has intellect and powers that, in this world, are second only to God Himself. Immediately he envisions a plan that, if successful, could change the destiny of everything God has created, especially those two humans He loves so much.

Remembering the words God spoke before this creation began, *"...There shall be no separation for those who receive My Love, for I shall establish My loved Ones from everlasting to everlasting...",* Satan sees a direct path for his sinister attack. First, he must entice the two humans to disobey God's direct commandment and eat the fruit of the tree of knowledge of good and evil. Second, if his intuition is correct, there will be another very special fruit in this garden of God, one that carries with it the reward of obedience, even eternal life. Eating this fruit of eternal life while being in the state of dis-obedience could forever seal their fate, locking them in an eternally unredeemable sinful condition, something Satan himself knows all to much about.

Focusing his attention, he initiates the first step of his evil attack. Zikeet says to the woman with an almost laughable arrogance, "I know this tree, you will not surely die." As they are talking, Zikeet begins moving slowly, subtly leading Eve closer and closer in the direction she had pointed to the middle part of the garden. Eve, fascinated with finding a creature in the garden that could speak to her in vocal communication, is unaware of the path that she is following as Zikeet continues to increase the pace.

Now struggling to keep up with the creature, Eve calls out, "Zikeet wait! What do you mean we shall not surely die?" Still moving quickly, Zikeet replies, "God knows that in the day you eat of it your eyes will be opened." Not understanding what he means, Eve questions, "Our eyes? But our eyes are open, I can see very clearly." Zikeet stops for a moment, and with a condescending arrogance, he explains, "Not with vision from your physical eyes," he says, "but your mind shall be opened and filled with all kinds of knowledge." The light now striking the face of this serpentine-like creature briefly reveals the empty blackness of his eyes as he cunningly slips back into the obscurity of the forest.

Continuing to lead Eve further into the middle of the garden, he begins to present even more enticing conversation. "God knows that in the day you eat of it you will become like gods." Again, he pauses, and for another brief moment he casts his gaze upwards, as if lost in some past experience, and continues to speak in whispering tones of animosity, "God is a jealous God! Not permitting any other gods to exist......for fear of competition I suppose!" Zikeet is startled back to the present as Eve shouts, "Become like God?" "Yes, like God!" exclaimed Zikeet in frustration. "I do not understand, we were made in the very image and likeness of God," Eve replies.

Zikeet, turning his head, and with a beguiling tone, speaks to Eve, "Yes, Adam was made in God's image and likeness, but you were made from Adam in his likeness."

To separate and deceive one of the two humans is still his primary objective. Sowing false seeds of discontentment is still Satan's first weapon of choice.

Now struggling to keep Zikeet in sight, Eve pushes through the dense foliage of the forest to reveal a beautiful grassy meadow. As she looks for Zikeet, she is taken by the calm serenity of this place. Something about it seems so familiar. Suddenly she realizes, this is the central part of the garden of God, the place of their beginning. She remembers being here only once before, but it was with her husband Adam and God Himself. It is here, under this tree God called the "Tree of Life", where God formed Adam from out of the dust of the ground, then God formed her from out of Adam. She remembers opening her eyes for the first time and seeing them both, face to face. Here under the Tree of Life is the very place of their beginning.

The subtle, slithering movement of the reptilian-like creature again catches her eye. Eve exclaims, "Wait, I don't understand. Why are we here?" Leading her further into the midst of the garden, Zikeet is now resting in the branches of a particularly massive tree; in fact, it is the only tree of its kind in all of the garden of Eden. He calls out to Eve, "Over here, come quickly and I will explain." Hurrying to meet him, Eve is overwhelmed by the size and beauty of this most unique tree. Even Zikeet seems small in its shadow. It is then she remembers once again the instructions of God just after they were created; this is the only tree of its kind, the only thing in all of God's creation forbidden to them.

Zikeet, sensing Eve's hesitation, continues to distract and draw Eve's attention by admiring the unmatched beauty of the fruit of this tree. "The fruit from this tree will make you equal in knowledge with both Adam and God," he states with a convincing boldness.

Though she is increasingly uncomfortable being so near this forbidden tree, she now begins to feel a strange sensation, one of irrational curiosity that seems so strong as to override even her own sense of obedience. Eve is now beginning to ponder what Zikeet was insinuating. She inquires once more, "Equal in what knowledge?" Zikeet, now holding the fruit of the tree before Eve, replies "All the knowledge of Good and Evil." Eve responds, "All of knowledge, what of gaining more knowledge could be evil? I know of no such thing!" Becoming suspicious, Eve inquires further, "Zikeet are you attempting to deceive me in this conversation?" Presenting the fruit in an enticing way, Zikeet says, "Not at all, see how I am holding this fruit and death has not come, neither shall I die from eating it." Holding the fruit closer to Eve and into the light, its unmistakable uniqueness is fascinating. Zikeet presses Eve further. "Take it now, you eat of this pleasant and good fruit and see for yourself that I speak good words." He continues, "Give it to your husband also and you both shall see and know; only then will you become equal with Adam and both of you will become equal with God."

Eve, still frozen in cautious hesitation, sits under the tree and begins to contemplate all that Zikeet has said.

Beyond the forks of the river at the edge of the garden, Adam stops. Noticing Eve is not walking with him, he begins to call out her name. While walking back in the direction where they had last been together, Adam notices something very different and strange. The sky above the middle of the garden is turning darker and churning with what appears to be black menacing clouds. Adam is mesmerized by this new climatic event as he continues calling for his wife Eve.

As the darkening sky above appears to be growing larger with every rotation of the unusual black clouds, something inside is pushing him with an overwhelming concern for his wife. With his heart pounding like never before, Adam now begins to run towards the middle of the garden.

Meanwhile, the subtle and persuasive nature of Zikeet is proving to be effective. Could Zikeet be telling her the truth? Eve considers what has been presented: The tree is pleasant to the eyes, and it's fruit seems good for food, and gaining knowledge is desirable. Eve, totally unaware of the changes happening in the atmosphere above her, is completely focused on the beauty of this tree and the potential benefits of its fruit. While still observing Eve, Zikeet notices Adam, who is quickly approaching them. Hurriedly, Zikeet rushes to entice Eve by taking a bite of the forbidden fruit himself. "Take just one little bite Eve, see I have tasted it and it is very, very good and I am certainly not dead!"

Now in a full sprint, Adam sees Eve nearing the fruit that was forbidden, he screams with all his might, "Eve No!"

So compelling was the deceptive influence of Zikeet that Adam's screams go unheard. As Adam approaches, Zikeet disappears into the thickness of the surrounding forest. Undetectable in the lush greenery of Eden's vegetation, the Prince of Darkness is waiting and watching for the inevitable outcome of his deceitful efforts.

Adam reaches out and grasps Eve by the shoulders and exclaims, "What are you doing here! This is the Tree of death. Do you not remember how I told you it is forbidden to eat of it or even touch it?" Eve tells of her conversation with Zikeet and how he appeared to be wise and knowledgeable concerning this tree. She explains how he said this fruit is actually very good and can make them both wise. Adam, in an obvious state of bewilderment replies, "Zikeet, who is Zikeet?" Adam continues to question, "God brought one of each kind of creature before me. Whatsoever I named them, God established for each one that name. I tell you I do not know of a creature named Zikeet in all this place." Immediately Adam begins looking diligently around the area for this creature Zikeet, all the while, Eve continues to look intensely at the fruit. It indeed appears to be good for food, just as Zikeet had said (after all, he took a bite and did not die!), it was pleasant to the eyes, and wisdom is good and something to be desired. Then, taking a deep breath, Eve took the fruit and ate.

So wonderfully different was the taste, that Eve immediately offered it to Adam her husband. Observing that death did not come as God had said, he listens to the pressing voice of his wife whom he loves. Unwilling to disappoint her, Adam takes of the fruit from Eve's hand and did eat as well.

At that moment, as immediate as the sensation of tasting the fruit is realized, the glory of God's creation begins to fade as the once innocent eyes of both of them begin to dim.

For the first time, they see only what human eyes can see. Eden is unrecognizable and dramatically different. Everything around them, all of Creation, once vibrant and brilliant in glorious heavenly splendor, appears now as only a shadow of what they remember. Suddenly, like a flash of light, they see the silhouette of something leaping from the trees. The insidiously tarnished appearance, only briefly visible, rapidly disappears into the blackness of the clouds above them. Disoriented, they hear a voice shouting from out of the darkness, "How does it feel to be like gods!"

With the first phase of his sinful scheme complete, Satan knows time is of the essence. Satan must act before the shock and confusion of the moment begins to subside. Quickly he moves to the tree Eve called the "Tree of Life". Resting in the branches of this beautiful tree, he calls out to Adam and Eve once more, "Hurry, you must eat from this tree, it will give you everlasting life." Eve immediately recognizing the voice of Zikeet, realizes the deceptive intention of his enticements as she begins to weep bitterly. Laughing and taunting them

Satan speaks once more, "Quickly, you must eat from this tree or you shall surely die!" Suddenly another stark realization of their disobedience, they themselves are no longer covered with beautiful robes of innocence. Now they stand naked before each other in shameful remorse. Quickly, they look away as Adam asks, "What should we do to cover ourselves?" Eve, looking around at the nearby trees replies, "Gather leaves from the fig trees." So the two humans tie fig leaves together and make for themselves coverings to hide their nakedness.

Only moments before, the two were robed in the glorious beauty of pure innocence, but now they stand in pitiful coverings hurriedly knit together from tree leaves.

Bewildered by the sudden events, Eve tearfully exclaims, "How can a fruit so desirable and so tasteful result in such consequences?" Still hidden in the darkness above, Satan speaks softly with a tauntingly sinister tone, "Why are you sad? Not quiet the result you expected? Sneering and laughing he continues adding insult to injury, "No matter, soon you both shall see how God Himself truly feels about you!"

Adam, in a state of shock and confusion, stands speechless. The forbidden fruit so irresistible and wonderfully sweet, was truly enjoyable, but only for a moment. Now that one moment of pleasure has quickly turned into a bitter and empty feeling of distressing disillusionment.

Standing in the disappointing realization of their actions, the next sound they hear is far more terrifying. Immediately, they hear the sound of the Lord God walking in the garden. Adam with Eve quickly hide themselves deep among the foliage and trees of the garden. Now aware of their first act of disobedience, the two remain hidden and shaking uncontrollably as the Lord God Himself approaches closer. Then the Lord God calls out to Adam, "*Where are you?*" Adam with a trembling voice responds, "I heard you coming in the garden, and I am hiding and ashamed." God replies, "*Tell me why you are hiding and ashamed*". Adam reluctantly replies, "I am ashamed and hiding because I have become naked." And the Lord God said, "*Who told you that you were naked? Have you eaten from the tree of which I commanded you that you should not eat?*" Then Adam, lowering his head said, "The woman whom You gave to be with me, she gave me of the tree, and I ate." And the Lord God said to Eve, "*What is this you have done?*" Eve says, "Yes, I did eat, but the creature Zikeet! He deceived me!"

Then the Lord God clearly seeing the creature they called Zikeet, compels it into the open area of the garden and into His pure light revealing in full the creature.

God, speaking to the creature, exclaims "*It is a clever disguise for one who is not of this world.*" Again the Lord God speaks aloud, "*This is the influence of My enemy, the one fallen and cast down from the court of Heaven.*" Then Adam exclaims, "That is a Leviathan!" The Lord God speaking to Adam and Eve says, "*This is a Leviathan in appearance only. It is the whisperer of temptations and the father of all lies in disguise. This is the Devil called Satan!"*

The Lord God using only His breath, removes the dark clouds in the sky above the garden area revealing the wicked instigator. Satan is compelled into the light and is now seen clearly as the tarnished fallen Angel once known as Lucifer.

The Lord God turns to the creature Eve called Zikeet and speaks aloud, *"Because you have yielded to this tempter, you are cursed more than all cattle, and more than every beast of the field. On your belly you shall go, and you shall eat dust all the days of your life."* Instantly the judgement of the Lord God transforms the once majestic and unique creature into a smaller serpentine form having no external appendages. The only means of movement is to shift it's now cylindrical body from side to side in the dust of the earth as it shamefully slithers away. Because it had listened to the whispers of Satan, the Lord God also stopped up its ears to no longer be tempted by audible sounds again.

Then the Lord God looking intently back at Satan proclaims: *"As a demonstration of My Great Love for this world, I will plant a Seed in My chosen people that shall in due time be the first fruit of eternal life. And I will put enmity between you and the woman, and between you and her Seed; Mercy I have willed from before the foundation of the world; He shall deliver forever My favored ones from the curse that has been birthed within your heart this day. It is He who will sit at My right hand of power having the fullness of the Godhead bodily. You shall bruise His heel, but He shall one day crush your head!"*

Pausing only for a moment, the Lord God continues to speak, *"From the foundation of this world I have willed that your pride shall become frustrated by the humbleness of my favored ones. My power shall be revealed in their weaknesses; Your strength will be subdued by their simple action of Faith in Me."*

Turning His attention to the woman, the Lord God said: *"I will greatly multiply your sorrow and your conception; In pain you shall bring forth children; Your desire shall be for your husband, and he shall rule over you."*

Now face to face with Adam, the Lord God speaks, *"I made you to be both Governor and Guardian over all the earth, to tend and keep this place and its inhabitants. I gave you the ability to choose obedience, and the strength to protect Eden's most prized creation, Eve your wife. In this single action of weakness and disobedience, sin and its influence shall be a curse to all of creation."*

The Lord God continues, *"Because you have chosen to heed the voice of your wife instead of My commandment, and have eaten from the tree of which I commanded you, saying, 'You shall not eat of it': Cursed is the ground for your sake; with hard labor you shall eat of it all the days of your life. Both thorns and thistles also shall come forth increasing your labor, and you shall eat the herb of the field. In the sweat of your face, you shall struggle and eat bread till you return to the ground. For out of the ground you were taken. From dust you were formed, and to dust you shall return."*

As the two humans stand helplessly in silent restraint, the Lord God turns his eyes towards the meekest of all the animals in the garden which the Lord God had made. With the same loving compassion as on the day He first created them, the Lord God reached out and took two pure spotless lambs from the first born of the flock of sheep. Holding the two lambs tenderly in His arms, the Lord God lifted them up and blessed them with His kiss.

At that moment, there came a light of such brilliance and luminosity that the two humans were unable to look upon what was happening. The intensity of the moment caused them to cover their faces and fall to the ground. As quickly as the light flashed, the humans feel the gentile hand of their Lord God lifting them up from the ground. As their eyes slowly opened and their vision cleared, they noticed that the two little lambs were no longer there.

Adam, awestricken and still trembling with fear from what just happened, mustered the courage to speak asking the Lord God, "What happened to the two Lambs?"

The Lord God, looking deeply into the fearful eyes of the humans, stretched forth His arms to reveal crimson red blood dripping from the palms of His hands.

The Lord God answered and said, *"There was no other way. Alone you could never provide an acceptable atonement for yourselves.*

Because you have disobeyed the only commandment I had given you,
sin has now entered your heart and defiled you.

The Lord God continues to speak, "*The innocent blood that once*
flowed through your veins has been contaminated and there is only one
cure for this sickness which otherwise would forever separate you from
Me. Innocent, pure blood must be shed. For without the shedding of
innocent blood, there can be no remission, no forgiveness of your sin."

His eyes now glistening with compassion, the Lord God looks
intensely at the two bewildered humans and says, "*It is by my will*
that a spotless Lamb shall become a necessary substitution for you and
suffer your penalty. So, by His innocent blood as substitution for your
guilt, the wages of sin shall be paid, and you both shall be redeemed."

As the full cost of their disobedience settles crushingly upon
them, Adam and his wife Eve collapse to the ground shedding tears
of true repentance in remorseful regret under the shameful weight
of their sin. Then the Lord God wraps His arms around the two
humans tenderly holding them as they weep.

Once again, they feel the gentile touch of the mighty hands of
their Lord lifting them to their feet. He removes their pitifully insuf-
ficient garments which they had hurriedly knit together from fig
tree leaves, and made them new clothes like robes resembling lamb's
skins. The Lord God placed the new robes upon both Adam and
Eve, covering their bodies completely from shoulders to feet so that
nothing of themselves could be seen save their faces.

With this first sacrificial act of grace and mercy, the Lord God has clothed both Adam and Eve in garments of white wool, as pure white and spotless like His very own appearance. Though the sacrifice of blood does remove the penalty of sin, the effect or "wage" of sin is always death. The physical effects of sin upon all the inhabitants of the new world will continue.

The special relationship between the two humans and the Lord God has been undeniably altered. God will no longer walk physically and visibly with man, but He will be present in spiritual manifestations and signs, recognizable only through the eyes of faith. By the covering of man's sin with innocent blood, the Lord God gives hope in a future re-establishment of both a physical and spiritual relationship between the Creator and His creation as it was in the beginning. The unmerited love of God toward humanity has now become evident.

Though the human world and the heavenly world are no longer compatible, truly God so loves this world.

The Eviction

*H*overing discreetly in the atmosphere above the earth, Satan observes the gracious action of the Lord God towards the two easily manipulated humans.

This unmerited act of mercy further infuriates the already demented state of his animosity. His jealousy boils to volcanic proportions as he realizes the personal relationship he once enjoyed with God, has now been focused upon these two humans called Adam and Eve.

His first attempt to destroy humans has failed. He underestimated the love that God has for these creatures, however he will not make that mistake again. Satan has begun a tragedy that will continue to bring damage and destruction to the new creation of God, and more importantly opportunity for victory over this coming threat God called the "Seed."

As he ponders his next move, Satan recalls with precision the words God spoke about this Chosen One to come:*"a spotless Lamb; His innocent, pure blood must be shed; For without the shedding of innocent blood, there can be no remission, no forgiveness of sin."* Pondering these descriptive words, "A spotless Lamb," and "by His innocent blood," Satan, reasoning with a supernatural intelligence, pieces together the true and full meaning of what God has said.

The Lamb is not an animal but the offspring of a human, "the Seed of a woman." As God has indicated, His sacrifice of two innocent lambs is only a "covering" of sins. Not until the coming of the Seed will full and final restitution and removal of their sin be possible.

Satan now understands that the blood of animals offers only a temporary protection from the law of God and His demand for righteousness and holiness. Again, he remembers God's words, *"For without the shedding of innocent blood, there can be no remission, no forgiveness of sin."* The only way to provide a full and lasting "Salvation" would be to somehow provide a single sinless sacrifice having perfectly pure blood. But to be accepted under the law, it would have to be the blood of a human since it was the humans who sinned against God.

With this understanding, Satan believes he knows how to achieve his goal of victory. He must continue to infect the bloodstream of all humans and prevent any opportunity to produce a human "Seed" with pure innocent blood. Knowing that God alone holds the keys of life and death, Satan has only limited power to affect the lives of humans and this only with God's permission.

With his true form having been revealed, he will be easily recognized and remembered by Adam and Eve. He must once again alter his tactical approach so he might continue to deceive and defile every facet of God's new creation. Satan realizes that all future attempts to corrupt humans must be done in shadows of deception, blurring the lines of morality and forever confusing the truth. His weapons will be doubts, fears, uncertainties, trimmed in fictitious superficial illusions all whispered into the ears of those who will listen. A new disguise will also be needed. To avoid detection, darkness has become his realm as he pridefully lays claim to its throne. In self-appointed arrogance, he presents himself as its ruler supreme. Masquerading as an "Angel of Light," the flame of jealousy and hatred will burn forever in this new Prince of Darkness.

The new earth is a large place, in order to cover the entire globe, he would need followers of his own. Though he has spiritual beings under his command, demons and fallen Angels of sort, it is more effective, even preferred, to use those of this world in order to carry out all his devious schemes. Since he has no power within himself to create, his power will manifest by deceiving and misleading those who become weak in their faith and love for God.

By causing the first two humans to sin, he is convinced that this will be his continuing strategy, and become a source of anguish and pain for God Himself.

He recalls how effective the methods used in Heaven were on those holy beings. How by simply providing a distraction and offering them an intriguing option, they turned their faces from God and sealed their fate. He reasons, if it worked on Holy Angels in Heaven, it most certainly would work on mortal humans in this lower place called Earth. He must now wait for mankind to multiply.

For now, Satan must remain vigilant and observe every woman born hereafter. Certainly, a woman chosen to deliver this "Savior of humanity" will be unique and distinguished among average women. Gathering his legions of demons, he instructs them to carefully observe every female born until they find the one through whom the prophesied Seed shall come. Satan elaborates further offering his presumptuous details: "Watch for a woman who will appear as if clothed with the sun, and the moon under her feet." He adds one final detail of his arrogant imagination, "She will most certainly be of royal descent; an heiress to an earthly kingdom, having a magnificent crown appearing as though adorned with the stars themselves."

With his vast army of demons commanded to search out this woman, Satan knows it's only a matter of time until his demonic hoards find her. He needs only to wait and stand ready to completely devour this Seed Child the moment she gives birth. For an eternal supernatural being like Satan, time is only a temporary inconvenience. For now, this Prince of Darkness will keep watching for more opportunities to continue building his army of evil in preparation for the inevitable war that will someday decide forever who will be the final authority.

Having provided an atonement for the sin committed by the first two people and a cloak of animal skin covering their shame, the Lord God said, "*Behold, mankind has become like one of Us, to know good and evil. The tree of life must be protected lest he put out his hand to eat of it also and live forever in this fallen and sinful condition.*"

Once again, in a demonstration of His great love for the humans, God drives out the man and the woman from the Garden of Eden to prevent them from eating of the tree of life. God then placed mighty eternal heavenly beings called Cherubim at the gate of the garden, and a flaming sword which continually turns in every direction to guard the way to the tree of life.

With the gates to Eden's Garden now closed, all access for any created being in this world is forever denied. All pathways into Eden are no longer accessible or even visible, for God has hidden every aspect of this pristine place until the future fulfillment of His plan. Eden's garden exists only as fading memories in the minds of the two who once tasted of its fruit. Created to be the governors of this new world, Adam and Eve are now vagabonds, outcasts fleeing out of Eden. Forced to accept the reality of no longer being in the serene sanctuary of God's Garden, the unknown world around the two wanderers looms large and unsettling.

Now, a mere six steps from Eden, the two stop to catch their breath. With Eden's sanctuary faded from sight, a harsh fact of their present condition is further realized, they must seek both provisions and shelter for themselves. Looking around at the vast new landscape, Eve exclaims aloud, "Where are all the plants and trees?" Kneeling, Adam grasps a handful of soil. This ground is very dry and much harder, nothing like the soil found in Eden's Garden. He wonders if it will even be possible to cultivate it; will anything grow in such a vast, desolate land? Adam replies, "I don't know, Let's just keep walking."

Looking toward the horizon, the hills appear green with trees and other vegetation. "This way," Adam says, "The hills have trees, maybe we can find shelter there." Pressing wearily onward, this new environment begins to take its toll upon the two wanderers. Suddenly Eve falls to the ground, grasping her foot in pain as she shouts for Adam to help her. "What happened?" Adam asked. "My foot, it hurts!" exclaims Eve. Dropping to his knees, Adam examines her foot and notices something extremely strange. There's something dark dripping out of Eves foot. It's the color of crimson red. Immediately they remember the first moment they ever saw blood. It was when the Lord God showed them His hands after the sacrifice of the lambs.

Bewildered and frightened, Adam confesses, "I don't know what to do!" After a moment of wiping off the injured area of her foot, the cause of the injury is revealed. A long, sharp object, attached to a small stem or vine of some kind is stuck in the heel of Eves foot. No plant Adam was familiar with ever looked like this, at least not when they were still in the garden. Adam carefully removes the thorn from Eves foot, but the bleeding continues. Adam remembers, while running out of the garden, they had managed to keep some of the leaves that they initially used to cover themselves. Adam takes one of the leaves and wraps it around Eve's injured foot. Almost instantly after he applies it to the injured area, the bleeding stops. As the pain from the injury begins to subside, Eve remarks, "That is much better, thank you." Adam replies, "It was the leaves from the trees of Eden. There must be healing in them."

It was true, everything in Eden provided comfort and healing. In Eden's Garden, they never experienced pain or weaknesses of any kind. God had provided everything needed: climate, water, food, and perfect, protected health. Eden was like Heaven on the earth, a place of terrestrial perfection.

The continual rejuvenating effects, once unnoticed and natural while living in the garden of God, are now rapidly fading away. With each passing moment, they feel the demands of a body that is no longer regenerating. As a result of the curse of sin, they are now subject to physical fatigue and pain, and soon they will also feel the emotional distress that accompanies physical fatigue.

As God had forewarned them, disobedience brings the curse, and death is the inevitable result. Because of their sin, the newly created world they have been exiled into is also cursed. Even the few animals they saw, once friendly and comforting, now flee from their presence. All of this serves as a painful reminder of the immeasurable cost of their disobedience. The curse of sin brings death, not to them only, but to all of creation.

With Eve leaning upon Adam's arm, the two continue toward the trees in the distant hills, hoping to find a place of relief from the intensity of the sun.

With a parched, cracking voice, Eve whispers, "My throat and tongue are so dry, are there no rivers of water outside of Eden?"

In this environment, the temperature can vary significantly, and the sun is just another constant reminder of a paradise lost.

As evening approaches, they have finally reached the green hill country. Walking ahead, Adam looks and joyfully exclaims, "Eve there's water here!" Adam rushes back to help Eve to the spring and the two drink for the first time since they fled Eden. "The water tastes different," says Eve. Adam replies, "I have a feeling that everything is going to be very different here."

After washing the dust from his face, Adam grasps Eve's hand as the two stand desperately staring out over the vast unfamiliar land now surrounding them. Moving deeper into the hill country to escape the arid heat of the barren, desolate land they had just traversed, the two come upon a small opening in the side of a rocky hillside. With nightfall rapidly approaching, they agree to shelter in the cave for the evening. As the sun begins to fall below the distant horizon, the temperature soon follows, and once again another new experience. Facing the extreme heat during the day was an unexpected challenge, but now the cooling night air is proving to be equally uncomfortable. Huddling close together against the back of the cave wall, the two outcasts realize another useful quality of their fleece robes that the Lord God had made for their covering. The robes served as a protection from the intense heat of the sun during the day, and now as protection from the cold during the night.

At this moment, the two of them thanked the Lord God for His merciful provision! Their first day outside of Eden has proven to be uncomfortable, fearful, and fully exhausting.

The rising of the sun awakens the two weary exiles and brings with it the ending of the first full day and night outside of the garden of God. As Adam cautiously moves outside the sanctuary of the small cave, he feels a surprising warmth. It appears to be coming from the stones that earlier in the previous day were in the sunlight. The two begin to gather some of the warmer ones and stack them in a place where the sun would heat them throughout the rest of the day. Adam explains, "This should help keep us warmer during the cool nights."

With each moment comes new revelations, as well as new challenges. For the first time, they both feel an emptiness, it is the discomfort of hunger. In the garden of God, all manners of fruit were easily available. Now they must go searching for food, hoping that they will find something suitable to eat. While walking through the vegetation on a nearby hillside, Eve notices a spring of clear water flowing from beneath a large outcropping of rocks. Eve calls for Adam to come and see.

Growing all around the spring are trees ripe with fruits and nuts that are at least somewhat familiar to the two humans. As Adam carefully inspects each fruit-bearing plant, he finds the same type of sharp growths protruding from the vines surrounding the fruit itself. It is the same thing that just the day before he had removed from Eve's foot. Then the words of the Lord God return to him, "*Cursed is the ground for your sake; In toil you shall eat of it all the days of your life. Both thorns and thistles it shall bring forth for you, and you shall eat the herb of the field.*"

With a cautious yet understandable hesitation, they begin to sample the food. After finding it good to eat, they gathered enough for the day and returned to the cave.

Slowly the days turn into weeks and weeks turn into months as Adam and Eve are learning how to live off this new and difficult land. The work they once loved and found joyful in Eden's garden is now strenuous and very demanding. They find it frustrating to work in this harsh, unpredictable environment. Weeds and vines constantly invade the garden area around the spring and must be removed continually. The changes in the weather are sometimes dramatic and hard to predict. The temperature varies throughout the season and sometimes the wind is very strong and damaging to the crops.

With each passing day, the two outcasts begin to learn how to cultivate and grow more of the fruit and plants they depend on for food. They are noticing patterns in the environment and watching the signs in the sky to better prepare for planting and harvesting.

Though living is much more difficult in this environment, the first two humans are beginning to feel more confident and even more productive in this new world. Everything they need to survive seems to be available somewhere in this land.

With each passing day, Adam and Eve notice that this land, while incomparable with the splendor of Eden's garden, has an undeniable beauty of its own. Each morning begins with a spectacular sunrise painting the sky in the most wonderful colors, which seems to awaken all the earth. The birds become active and begin to sing as flowers open in a glorious display of a new day. Soon, they both begin to feel the attraction for each other that first began to flourish in the day they were in the garden of Eden. Even here, they find great consolation in simply being together.

At the close of one particularly productive day, Adam and his wife Eve sit together in what has become a favorite resting place for the two. It is a large rock facing eastward, located higher up on a nearby hillside, that overlooks the lush green landscape in the direction of the now inaccessible garden of Eden.

As the sun continues to fall lazily toward the western horizon, the retiring of another day produces brilliant displays of fleeting yet spectacular beauty. However, something about this evening seems even more captivating. With the setting of the sun, the warmth of the day soon follows suit. As the chill of the encroaching night begins to fall, Eve moves even closer to her husband. Following their eviction from Eden's Garden, their feelings for each other had become an unaffordable luxury in light of the necessities of survival.

Adam, feeling the desire of his wife, gently embraces her in his arms. For the first time since their eviction from the garden of God, the two begin feeling the closeness they began to experience in Eden. Remembering the moment God Himself first presented them to each other and pronounced them husband and wife, it would be this night in the most intimate fashion, that the ceremonial proclamation made by God would be consummated.

In the following weeks since their first night of intimacy, Adam notices that Eve has been strangely preoccupied and more distant, especially the last few days. One evening, as Adam returns from working in the field, he is surprised to see that Eve has prepared a special meal. He also notices that her appearance is different, and she is smiling today more than he remembers since their expulsion from the garden. After they have eaten, Eve sits before Adam and shares the reason for her lifted spirit. Eve is going to have a child. The two now rejoice as Adam sings praises to God who has smiled upon them and blessed them. The evening comes and the morning brings with it a new day. It is a day filled with anticipation and renewed hope.

Over the next few weeks, Adam and Eve prepare for their soon coming child. Their excitement is twofold. They are very thankful that the curse did not remove their ability to have children and multiply, and excited to have another person on the earth in addition to themselves.

When the fullness of her time had come, Eve bore Cain and said, "I have received a man child from the LORD!" She bore again, this time his brother Abel.

As the years passed, Eve also bore other children. The family of Adam and Eve began to prosper in this new world. Eventually, some would help in the fields under the direction of Cain, the first born of Adam's sons, and others would tend to the animals that Adam and his second born son Abel had domesticated to help them survive. Oxen are tamed and used to plow the soil and tend to the fields. Sheep are raised to provide wool for clothing and other woven fabrics. Some of Adam's children also learn to make large coverings from the woven fabric to use as shelters and dwellings.

Since the very first season, Adam established a tradition. Just after the first harvest, Adam would take their children and walk to a favorite spot atop of a nearby hill and stand upon the large rock facing eastward in the direction of the now hidden location of Eden's Garden. There he would place offerings of the first fruits from all their increase unto the Lord God. After the time of offering, Adam would remain alone and wish for forgiveness of the sin that caused the separation and broken relationship with God. With each passing season, Adam hopes that maybe this year God would receive them back into Eden's garden and restore their personal relationship, even walking with them as before.

One season, upon returning from the offering of first fruits, Eve questions Adam privately asking, "When should we tell the children about Eden and the reason why we can no longer speak to God face to face?" Adam stands up, looking at Eve, and says, "They know of no other life but this, to learn about Eden would be cruel and of no profit to them, and most certainly they will hate us both!" Eve speaks again, "I just don't want to have any secrets from our children, they need to know who they should trust in this world. I don't want any of them to be deceived as we were." Adam abruptly interrupts, "You mean as you were!" As Adam leaves, Eve weeps bitterly and tearfully whispers, "How much longer must I suffer this guilt within my heart?"

Working nearby in one of the fields, is Cain, the firstborn son of Adam and Eve. He is a gifted farmer and very talented in management of the land and crops. Being the eldest son, he has much of the responsibility of providing food for the growing family. Stopping to wipe the sweat from his face, Cain hears a strange sound coming from in the sky. He stops working for a moment and peers upward to see two birds as they appear to be struggling over a small tuff of wheat. The one bird is larger and appears to be overpowering the smaller one. As the two birds continue to struggle over the stalk, they plummet to the ground. The larger bird, standing over the smaller one, takes the piece of wheat and then flies away. The smaller bird, obviously injured from the struggle, could no longer fly away. Cain's concentration is broken when he hears his mother Eve standing on the far side of the field, calling to him. "Do not forget, you must gather together your brother Abel's flock, he is with his father on the mountain today," Eve shouts. This does not sit well with Cain. Why is Abel with their father again? Why should he have to do Abel's work as well as his own? After all, he is the first born son, not Abel. Abel provides no food for the family, he only watches and tends the sheep. Cains heart begins to burn with jealousy concerning his brother Abel. Looking back at the struggling smaller bird, Cain imagines for a moment how he would like to overtake his brother and prove his rightful position as the firstborn son.

Circling high above the land, there is another presence which is unseen. Satan resides in the atmosphere around the earth where he is the reigning Prince and Power of the air. He has been carefully observing the humans, patiently waiting for any opportunity to continue his deceitful work.

In truth, he is the most powerful of all created beings in this new lower world of earth. He carefully planted his damnable seed of rebellion in Eden, first with Adam and Eve. Now moving all around the earth, he is seeking anyone who might yield to his whispering lies and deceitful intentions.

Observing the discontentment now visible in Cain's countenance, Satan sees his first opportunity in this new arena. Remembering the words of God and how the "Seed" from the woman would someday crush his head, Satan continues his evil scheme to cut off and destroy this prophesied coming opponent. Beginning with the firstborn children of the first two humans, Satan vows to corrupt every one born from this day forward until he has destroyed this prophesied "Seed" and established himself as the only ruler over all of creation.

The Consequences

*N*ow Abel is a keeper of sheep, but Cain is a tiller of the ground. And in the process of time, as was their common practice, Cain brings an offering of the fruit of the ground to the Lord. But the Lord is not pleased with Cain and rejects his offering. A short while later, Abel also brings an offering of the firstborn of his flock and of their milk. And the Lord is pleased with Abel and receives his offering.

Cain is very angry, and his countenance reflects the discontentment that is in his heart. So the Spirit of the Lord speaks to Cain and asks, *"Why are you angry? And why has your countenance fallen?"* Cain says, "It's Abel, It's always Abel! Abel is always preferred before me! I was the first born and I do more work, still he is everyone's favorite. Now even you have chosen him over me." Then the Lord says to Cain, *"Not so, for if you do well, do I not accept you also?"* Cain replies, "No one shows any appreciation for all the work I do. No one ever acknowledges me. Everyone thinks Abel is great because he tends to the sheep and provides the wool for our clothing and coverings. Tell me, which is more important, to have food enough to eat, or to have coverings made from animal hair!"

The Lord says, *"Hear me well Cain, your works can be considered good, but if the contents of your heart are evil, sin lies at the door of your heart."* In frustration, Cain replies to the Lord, "I have done everything you asked and still my work is not good enough!" Once again, the Lord speaks to Cain and says, *"My acceptance of your offering is not based upon the kind or quality of your works, but a condition of the purity and intention of your heart."* Cain continues in his contention with the Lord, "How can I be of a pure heart when I am being treated so unfairly!" Then the Lord chastens Cain and says, *"Be careful! For I will not continue to strive with you concerning this matter. Do not be blinded by sinful pride. It is sinful desire that corrupts you, but you have the ability to choose good over evil."*

When the Lord had finish speaking these words, His Spirit departed from Cain. Knowing the words that the Lord speaks are true, Cain understands that what the Lord expects of them all is a pure and sincere heart. Cain considers all the Lord has said, then in a moment of frustration, he scatters the fruit from his offering and turns to leave from the altar of the Lord.

Now Cain has decided to plant a new vineyard in the land that is further to the east from the main camp of Adam. Cain thinks that if he could just get far enough away from Abel, that he could somehow deal with his life's circumstances better.

In the days following the Lord's refusal of Cain, he continues to hide the animosity he has in his heart for his brother Abel.

Growing more and more intolerant of everyone, Cain begins to withdraw even further from the family. Soon, even his parents begin to notice a difference in Cain's attitude, particularly concerning Abel his brother.

Deeply concerned with the strife now prevalent in the heart of Cain, Adam sought counsel with his son. Adam called upon one of the young women who seemed particularly fond of Cain, to deliver a message that Adam desired to meet with him as soon as possible. Having received the message of his father Adam's desire to meet with him, Cain hurried back to the central camp. As Cain entered the camp, he notices his younger brother Abel leaving Adam's tent heading back toward the fields where the flocks of sheep are feeding. Cain, now carefully avoiding any potential contact with his brother, waits for Abel to be well outside the camp before approaching the tent of Adam his father.

Upon entering the tent, Adam greets Cain, "My son." Cain replies, "My Father." As the two embrace, as is the normal custom, Adam speaks again, "Please come and let us reason together." Moving toward the center part of the tent, Cain notices his mother Eve standing at the table where, in his youth, the family would sit and have meals and fellowship together. For a moment, time seems to stop as memories of the past overtake the present. Cain recalls the earlier days when it was only the four of them. He remembers how his younger brother Abel was always looking up to him and how he, being the stronger of the two, felt very protective of his brother Abel.

One memory stands out above the rest. Cain remembers the days when the two of them would play together in the hills just beyond the camp. The two had a favorite game of sort that they enjoyed when time permitted. It was a game of hiding and seeking. Abel would cover his face first while Cain would hide somewhere in the wooded area near the fields of tall grass. On one particular day, after all the chores were finished, Abel wanted to play hide and seek. Cain, noticing it was later in the day, tried to convince Abel to wait until the morning when they would have more time to play. Abel continued to plead with his older brother to play just one quick game. As Cain looked into the yearning eyes of his little brother, he reluctantly agreed. Cain recalls the pure excitement of Abel, and remembers the joy within his own heart seeing his brother so happy. In truth, Cain really wanted to play too! After all, he truly loved Abel and enjoyed spending time with his younger brother.

As the two brothers went running out of the camp, Abel insisted that this time he be the first to go and hide. Cain agreed, knowing this would guarantee a short game, since he could always find Abel quickly.

There was a special place where they would always begin this game. A very large tree stood alone atop of a hill adjacent to the area where the fields and wooded area was located. This tree was their favorite place. It had large limbs extending outward, which made it easy to climb. Many times, after they would play, the two brothers would climb up into the tree and relax upon one of its large branches. They had even taken sharp stones and carved their marks deep into the massive trunk, Cain's mark carved first and close beside it was Abel's. As was their custom when playing this game, the one hiding would be given a head start while the one seeking would lean against the tree and number the sheep in their father's flock before beginning their search.

So Abel went off to hide while Cain began to count. Shortly, Cain was off to begin the search. Now Cain knew his brother's normal habits and hiding places so he began looking in those areas first. Much to his surprise, Abel was not in any of the regular hiding places. Off in the distance Cain hears their mother Eve calling them home. He calls back in response and waits silently to hear the response from Abel. Hearing no response, Cain calls out to Abel, "The game is over, Mother is calling us home." Still, there is no response. Cain calls out again, "Ok, you win, now it's time to go home!" After what seemed to be a day's length of no response, Cain continues to call out to his brother Abel. With every moment of silence that passed, Cain's heart would beat faster with concern.

As Cain turned to watch the sun sinking toward the distant horizon, he could feel his hope fading into fear for his brother's safety.

Now in a full state of panic, Cain does the only thing he can think of, he sprints as fast as he can back to their camp for help. With the darkness of night rapidly approaching, time is of the essence. What started as a harmless game has now become a frightening situation.

Over the next few hours, the family of three canvased the area where Abel and Cain had been playing. Stopping for a moment to assess the situation, the weight of reality begins to settle upon Cain as he collapses into his mother's arms. Cain in deep tears of repentance exclaims, "It is all my fault, I should not have agreed to play so late in the day!" Eve, together with her husband Adam, lovingly console Cain. They continue the search, spreading out farther from the camp, farther than the two boys have ever ventured while playing before. As darkness settles heavily upon the searchers, the torches Adam and Eve are using for light begin to fade. The unavoidable decision is made to return home while they could still find the way and wait for the first light of morning. Cain recalls this to be the longest night of his young life.

The next morning, with the first light of a new day comes a renewed determination to find Abel. The three leave the camp and hurry back to the place they had last searched the night before. They continue their searching as each one taking turn would call out for Abel then listen in hopeful silence. As they begin to move methodically into the trees towards the wooded mountainous area, Adam asks why they were playing so far from the camp? Cain replies they have never played this far away from home.

As the minutes turn into hours, the fears of the small family begin to grow even greater with concern for the safe return of Abel. Adam calls out once again for his son as the three searchers listen intently hoping for a response. Once again, the sun begins to sink toward the western horizon, and taking with it their hopes of finding Abel. Reluctantly, Adam says the words no one wanted to hear, "We must turn back and return home." Weeping, Eve collapses to the ground under the weight of the moment. Adam along with Cain reach to lift her to her feet when suddenly a weak, almost whimpering sound is heard. Frozen with hopeful anticipation, as to not even take another breath, they all listen intently in the direction of the sound. Again, they hear the sound, it was definitely a cry of some sort. Immediately Eve cries out to Abel in hopeful desperation. Now stronger with a renewed hope, the voice of Eve echoes through the hills. The three do not have to wait long for a recognizable response. With hearts lifted by a renewed hope, the three searchers begin running in the direction of the cry. With darkness rapidly approaching, Adam cautions both Eve and Cain concerning the rugged terrain they are now entering. In this landscape, the rocky hills are treacherously steep and potentially deadly.

Calling out once more, the three stand in motionless silence, as if frozen in time, waiting to hear any response. Unable to endure the deafening silence any longer, Eve cries out loudly, "Abel, please answer!" As the sound of Eve's voice echos through the rocky cliffs, fading with each reverberation, there is a faint but unmistakable answer, "Mother, over here!"

With hearts pounding, the first human family moves quickly but cautiously towards the sound. Adam is the first to reach the edge of a steep rocky ravine. Carefully peering over the edge, Adam sees his youngest son clinging perilously to a narrow ledge helplessly out of reach. Adam looking back at Eve and Cain with tearful eyes says, "He is too far down the cliff, I cannot reach him!" Immediately Eve takes Cain by the hand and rushes into the nearby forest gathering long thin vines. Upon returning, Eve says "Take these vines and tie them together". Hurriedly they tie the vines together to form a makeshift rope. Knowing that the vine rope would not support Adam or Eve, Cain, feeling responsible for this situation, quickly volunteers. Slowly, Adam lowers Cain down the steep cliff side to the ledge where Able is located.

Upon reaching his younger brother, Cain is overcome with tears of joy. Abel, though bruised and scraped from the fall, is alive! Quickly Cain ties the vine-rope around Abel and signals to their parents above to pull up the injured boy.

With Abel safely atop the precipice, both Adam and Eve fall to their knees and embrace their recovered child.

Weakened from the lack of food and water, Abel sits shivering in the cool night air watching as his parents lower the vine once more to bring his brother, and now his rescuer, back up the cliff. The safe return of his brother Abel once again emotionally overwhelms young Cain as his relief springs forth in tears of joy.

Many other things flood the mind of the now adult Cain as he stands in the moment of precious memories of a childhood filled with joy and brotherly love. What seemed to be years of reliving his past is only a few seconds. Cain is startled back to the present at hearing the voice of his mother Eve greeting him saying, "My son Cain, so good to see you this day." Cain responds, "My Mother, it is good to see you as well." Continuing on into the center room, which is the place of meeting, Adam is immediate with his purpose for Cain's visit, "What is this contention between you and your brother Abel?" Standing in silent but obvious animosity, Cain's heart instantly burns with jealousy at the very mention of Abel's name. Adam, seeing the response of Cain, says, "This contention between you and Abel must not continue for it is not pleasing to the Lord." Adam continues, "Do not wait until tomorrow, do not let the sun set this day until the fellowship has been restored between the two of you." Cain, with a heart hardened even more, immediately storms out from his father's presence. Adam, still seeking to restore his first two son's relationship, called again, this time for Abel.

Returning from out of the pasture where he had been watching the sheep, Abel enters the house of Adam and sits alone before his father. As Adam begins to speak, he reveals to Abel the things concerning the contention of Cain and how the resentment in Cain's heart is continually towards Abel. Adam questions Abel, "My son, is there any just cause for this strife of Cain towards you?" Abel, heartbroken and weeping, speaks aloud, "I have done nothing to justify his anger towards me, neither do I know of any reason for his jealousy." Abel, standing to his feet, makes a vow to his father Adam to speak to his brother Cain concerning this dispute, before the sun sets that very evening. So Abel leaves his father's house with his face set towards the eastern hillside where his brother Cain is working.

Standing just outside of Adam's tent is the young woman, who had grown very fond of the oldest son Cain. Having overheard the conversations between Abel and his father Adam, and wishing to gain more of Cain's favor, she runs ahead of Abel to the fields where Cain is plowing. When she arrives, she tells of all that she had overheard. Cain sending her away, shows her favor by making vows unto her.

As Cain continues his work, each passing moment seems to only intensify his anger toward Abel. Soon, Abel arrives to the fields where Cain is working and cries out to greet his brother, "Has the heat from the sun made my brother's heart dry and desolate for his younger brother Abel?" Cain continues to plow, ignoring the callings from his brother. Again, Abel speaks as he approaches closer to Cain, "I have brought water and bread enough for us both, come let us sit in the shade and reason together what manner of contention is between us." Cain stops his work, and stands for a moment in silent observation to notice if there is any other person in the area. Convinced they are alone, Cain makes a motion with his hand signaling to Abel to come forward into the shade of the trees where the two of them can sit.

Now Cain talks with Abel his brother, and Abel pleads with Cain to explain what is the matter of contention between the two of them. Cain becomes increasingly more frustrated and enraged at every word spoken by Abel. Standing to his feet, Abel walks to the opposite side of the tree they are sitting under and kneels near a particular area of the trunk. With a few gentle rubs of his hand, the long forgotten image carved into the tree is revealed. It is their marks they had placed there when they were children and the only two sons of Adam. "Those were wonderful days my brother," Abel says in soft tones of fondness. Cain responds, "Just bygone days, from a time best forgotten." "Good days and good, memories should never be forgotten," Abel replies. The relationship, once so cherished and memorialized, is now withering away as Abel makes one final plea for restoration.

Cain, fully committed to his adversarial position with Abel, stands abruptly and exclaims, "Enough! I am done with this concern, and I am done with you!" Realizing that Cain is not going to agree and resolve this issue, Abel rises from the place, shakes off the dust from his feet and begins walking back to the camp. While Abel turns to walk away, a strong wind arises stirring up the dust in front of Cain revealing what he had not noticed before. A large jagged stone now lays uncovered on the ground before him. The wind, seemingly whispering in his ear, fuels the flames of rage now building deep in the heart of Cain. In a moment of uncontrollable anger, Cain reaches down and grasps the stone firmly in his hands. Raising the stone high over the back of his brother Abel's head, Cain carries out the violent actions of the whispering deceiver speaking through the wind.

And it came to pass, when they were in the field, that Cain rose up in violent anger against Abel his brother and killed him.

With that single action of rage, the stirring wind immediately ceased, taking with it the whispering voice of the wicked instigator.

Now alone in the full realization of what he has done, Cain panics at the sight of the lifeless body of his brother. Thinking of nothing else, he drags the body of Abel into the nearby bushes and quickly covers it with dirt and leaves.

Hoping to escape his guilt, he begins to fabricate a story that might help to satisfy any questions that his father Adam might later ask.

When evening comes, and Abel does not return to the camp, as is his usual custom, Adam seeks out Cain to inquire of his brother's whereabouts. Cain tells his father about the meeting with his brother Abel and how they sat and talked in the shade of the trees. Then Cain lies to Adam and says that Abel left from the field where Cain was working, and he does not know where he could be. Cain continues in his deception and tells Adam that Abel had mentioned a missing lamb, lost earlier that morning in the western hills outside the camp, and that he may be searching for it still. It is well known that Abel loves his flock. This seems reasonable to Adam, so he eats and goes to sleep. Later, sometime after midnight, Cain's restlessness is magnified by the overwhelming guilt of his sin. He cannot flee from the images in his mind of the horrible actions he has committed against his brother Abel. Then, just before daybreak, the Spirit of the Lord speaks to Cain, "*Where is Abel your brother?*" Cain is shocked at the voice of the Lord and tries to ignore it. Again, the Lord persists, "*Where is Abel your brother?*" Cain says sharply, "I do not know, am I my brother's keeper?" The Lord speaks once more, "*What have you done? The voice of your brother's blood cries out to Me from the ground.*"

With the undeniable truth set before him, Cain breaks down before the Lord and weeps bitterly.

The Lord says to Cain, "*I warned you and foretold of the intention of the evil that was found in your heart. Because you would not hear and turn from your wickedness, you are cursed from the earth which has opened its mouth to receive your brother's blood from your hand. When you till the ground, it shall no longer yield its strength to you. A fugitive and a vagabond you shall be on the earth.*"

Cain, shouting aloud to the Lord, pleads, "My punishment is greater than I can bear! Surely You have driven me out this day from the face of the ground; how will I survive and what shall I grow to eat? Shall I also be hidden from your face? Without your protection, the others of my brother's family will search me out and will kill me!"

Startled awake as Cain's voice echoes throughout the camp, everyone rushes to see what is happening. Like a thunderous, mighty river, the voice of the Lord God is heard. God calls aloud for all living to hear the proclamation He is making to Cain. And the Lord says, "*Let it be known therefore, whoever kills Cain, vengeance shall be taken on him sevenfold.*" Confused at the Lord's proclamation and not understanding why anyone would want to kill Cain, Adam speaks aloud to ask God the meaning of this decree. The Lord God remains silent.

Adam and his family continue to watch in silence as the Lord God places a visible mark upon Cain as a protection against any who would seek to harm him.

Meanwhile, the family noticing Abel is still missing, begins to search for him. He has now been missing for almost a full day. Two of the sons of Adam go out searching the area in the eastern fields at the place Abel went to meet with Cain. While searching along the perimeter of the freshly plowed field, one of the two trips and falls to the ground. Rising to his feet and dusting himself off, he looks down to see what had caused him to fall. "A Stone," he exclaims. Reaching down, with intentions of throwing it further out of the field, he picks up the stone and sees a dark, moist stain on the sharp end. He shouts, "Brother, come quickly." Immediately the stain is recognized as blood. In sickening bewilderment, they drop the stone and feverishly begin to search the stubbled bushes around the edge of the field. They do not have to search but a short time before the body of their brother Abel is found. Their brother Abel had been shallowly buried near the field where Cain alone had been working.

Carrying the dead body of their brother along with the blood covered stone, the two enter the tent of their mother and father.

Overwhelmed with grief at the loss of their second born son, the obvious conclusion weighs heavily upon the hearts of Adam and Eve. With this sharp stone, Cain had killed his younger brother Abel. Now the full realization of God's statement and Cain's response is understood.

Beginning with one single act of disobedience in the garden of Eden, the consequences of sin continue to affect their new life and this new world.

As Adam and Eve weep uncontrollably while holding the body of Abel, Adam cries aloud, "Let it be known this day, I have lost two sons because of sin." Watching helplessly as their firstborn son Cain is driven away by the commandment of the Lord, Adam, still holding the lifeless body of Abel close to his chest, speaks aloud in agonizing words of despair, "Let the seed of Cain the fallen one never again be found within the family of Adam!"

So Cain leaves the camp of his father Adam, taking with him the young woman to whom he had pledged his vows. Some who were from the family of the young woman chose to depart with her and Cain.

As the small caravan of outcasts gather their belongings, the entire camp of Adam turns their faces away, refusing even to look upon those leaving. This is unmistakably a sign of remorseful rejection, signifying the ending of any previous relationship and disallowing any hope of future restoration.

After some time of traveling eastward, Cain and his small band of followers pitch their tents far beyond the camp of Adam and dwell in the land they called "Nod" which being translated means "Wandering".

Cain, once a successful farmer, struggles to produce crops in this harsh more desolate land. Surviving on the meager fruits and vegetation that could be found, the family of Cain are struggling in this new and difficult land.

As time progresses, the family of Cain continues to increase. Soon Cain and his wife conceive and bare a son, and they name him Enoch.

Cain is the first to begin to build structures made of stones and wood rather than tents made of woven fabric and cloth. Soon, these permanent structures become the first city. And it comes to pass that Cain calls the name of the first city after the name of his first son—Enoch.

And so begins the generations of Cain.

The Confession

*I*n a land filled with new experiences, the worse thing imaginable has come to pass. Life outside of Eden's Garden has proven to be difficult and now irreversibly tragic. Although physical pain has become an uncomfortable reality, the emotional pain of this day is experienced by the entire family of Adam and Eve.

The days following the tragedy prove to be equally challenging for both Adam and Eve. The one and only commandment of God given in Eden's haven has proven to be an inescapable truth: "*In the day you eat of the fruit, you shall surely die.*" Haunting words of painful regret that continue to ring loudly in the mind of both Adam and Eve. The judgement of their original sin of disobedience has now become a very painful realization. Death, because of their sin, has entered into the world of men, and it has begun with their own first-born sons.

As the shocking realization of their loss begins to settle, Eve is the first to succumb to the lingering effects of such emotional devastation. Now more than ever, Eve is struggling with the guilt and weight of feeling responsible for everything that has happened. Their initial loss was a tragedy, and her personal loss was heartbreaking, but to see the continual effects of sin is a devastating and overwhelming burden. Eve, feeling completely responsible for their situation, clings to her husband Adam, pleading with him to tell their story to the rest of the family, starting from the beginning. Confused and bewildered, having no real understanding of why these things have happened, all the family is called together.

Adam, heartbroken and tears falling, with Eve his wife standing by his side, begins to take the first step of true repentance by accepting the full responsibility for his own choice and actions. As his gaze directs everyone's attention to the eastern horizon, he points to an area where now only a few clouds in the sky and desert sands appear.

Adam begins to speak, "Where the sky touches the earth and the sun rises each day, lies an unseen land. It is a most Holy place guarded by Holy Beings. We can never enter this land for it is no longer accessible." Adam, now weeping, continues, "I must confess to you all that it was not always so." As those gathered to listen gasp in confusion at these words, they immediately begin to ask questions. What do you mean by "No longer accessible" and "It was not always so"? Was it ever accessible? If so, when was this possible and why is it no longer that way?

Adam, now trembling with remorseful grief, lifts his hands to pause the questioning as he continues his story, "Now, our land is harsh and is a land of struggle, but in the beginning, inside Eden, that unseen land, all was perfectly peaceful. There struggles, labors, pain, and even death itself did not exist." Adam continues his confession, "Inside of the land of Eden was a special place called the "Garden of God."

Someone within the crowd speaks up and asks the question, "How is it possible, you said no one can enter this place. How can you know so much about this unseen land?"

Now, feeling the full weight of his failure resting squarely upon his shoulders, he pauses for a moment and lovingly wraps his arms around his wife Eve and begins to confess directly to her, "Oh wretched man that I am, I have placed my sin upon my wife undeservingly. For she truly was deceived by the liar, but I Adam chose for my own self of my own desire." Adam looks deeply into Eve's tearful eyes and begs her forgiveness.

After a moment of the two embracing, Adam turns and faces the others and continues to speak, "All of this trouble and all of this hardship is the result of one man's sin." Everyone looking around at each other, agrees with him. They all perceive he is speaking of the deeds of Cain. Truly, grief and emotional distress had not been experienced like this before Cain's hideous act of violence. Some even begin to murmur words of judgement towards Cain, suggesting equal punishment for his deed. "Eye for and Eye" they begin to shout.

Adam, motioning again with his arms for silence, moves closer to the assembly. While they look deeper into his eyes, words of shocking revelation and truth are finally revealed. Adam continues to speak to the entire family, "For by one man's disobedience, sin has entered into the world of men, and it brings with it the penalty of death." Not yet fully understanding what is meant by this outpouring of emotional distress, one among those standing in the midst of the gathering speaks aloud, "Cain is the first man that has brought such despair and death to all of this world!" Others again join in aggravated agreement and begin to shout threatening words filled with anger and even vengeance against Cain, as well as all those who went with him.

Holding up his hands once more to signal silence among those gathered, Adam slowly sinking to his knees, exclaims plainly, "No, it is not Cain, I am the first man created by God, I am Adam, and I am that man."

As the crowd of relatives stand in stunned silence, all experience emotional responses of bewilderment, confusion, and disbelief at the unimaginable confession they are hearing now for the first time. Someone in the crowd breaks the awkward silence and speaks aloud asking for explanation and if Adam would continue to tell them more of what had happened back in the Garden of God.

Relieved of his long kept secret, Adam wipes the tears from his eyes and reaches out his hand to Eve his wife as the two embrace. Adam standing to his feet begins to speak, "Now it all happened like this, that in the beginning, God created all the Heavens and the Earth and everything you see now......."

So, Adam, with his wife Eve, begin to tell the story of the events of creation and the time they once enjoyed in Eden. After much weeping and confession, everyone gathered around the first man Adam and the first woman Eve, and they loved them even more.

As The Lord God from His throne, high above all creation, observed this wonderful moment of genuine repentance, He simply smiled and was once again pleased with the hearts of the first two humans whom He so loves.

Over the next 130 years, God blesses Adam and Eve and their family as they continue on together and prosper. Eventually, Adam and Eve have another son and they name him Seth, saying, "For God has appointed another seed in place of Abel, whom Cain killed." And as for Seth, to him also a son was born; and he named him Enosh, then men began to call on the name of the Lord in regularity, and in the form of personal prayers. Gathering for the purpose of acknowledging the sovereignty and goodness of God was becoming more and more common.

Through the process of time, it becomes the practice of the family of Adam that every seventh day is to be a day to worship the Lord

God who had created all things, and a day to rest from their labors just as God Himself had finished His creative works and rested on the seventh day. It is established as a sanctified holy day.

Having a common place to gather together and worship God as a family was Adam and Eve's common desire. With the help of some of the older sons, a tent of congregation was built. This tent would be a sanctified place for the people to assemble together and hear the stories of Adam and his wife Eve as they would retell their personal experience from the time of beginning until the present day. Adam, being the first man of this new world, was undeniably the first man to sin, and Cain was inarguably the second. However, there is one still silently present who contains within his own being the very seed of sin itself. Satan, the originator of disobedience and rebellion, is in every way the adversary of God and is now continually lurking in the shadows, waiting to influence the hearts and minds of those humans who will listen. Satan's first devastating attack on humanity, the garden deception of Adam and Eve, was soon followed by his careful cultivation of jealousy and rage in Cain producing the first act of murder. However, this is only the beginning of his master plan of attack. Satan vows to eternally oppose the very will of God in all things present and yet to come.

His plan since his fall is to corrupt the entire human race and squelch any possibility of the prophecy of God to be fulfilled. Where there are no humans, there can be no future "Seed" of a human woman to crush his head. His whispering lies and deceit have temporarily been derailed by the family of Adam and their dedicated devotion to serving and obeying the Lord God. However, there are others he can focus his reprobate efforts upon.

Far away to the east of the land where Adam dwells, Cain has been building a city and has filled it with his own descendants. Things in this land are very different and are influenced by a very different example, an unseen instigator of discontentment and pride. It is this seed of satanic influence that has taken root and fuels the flames of hatred that are now burning hot in the heart of Cain and all his descendants. There are no fond memories or stories of heritage shared here, only an obsessive distain for those who Cain still holds responsible for his abandonment and exile.

Given fully to the influential whispers of pride and arrogance, Cain has proclaimed that all those living in the land of Adam should be considered enemies. He further declares that all the lands of Adam rightfully belong to him, being the firstborn son, and therefore to all his descendants. Cain, obsessed with vengeance, vows to one day make right all of these wrongs.

Satan has been successful in the first most critical wave of his assault. It is an eternal truth that wherever the light of God illuminates, the seed of Satan can never prosper.

Satan's seed of discontentment and jealous pride thrives in darkness, but especially in the darkest most regions of the human heart. With his careful and continual cultivation, his evil seed of sin has now grown into a flourishing garden producing the fruit of his wicked intentions.

The battle ground has been established, humans hating humans is the unfortunate result of tasting the fruit of the Prince of Darkness. All things needed to cause this destructive division in the first human family, Cain has eagerly provided. Only one thing can produce failure now; the true light of God must be avoided at all costs.

Satan must continue to lead humans into the shadows of deception and confusion, keeping them from all light and truth. By feeding what is rapidly becoming an insatiable need to fulfill the desires of their flesh, Satan has established the central and most effective weapon in his arsenal. God has created humans with the freedom to choose good over evil. Satan speaks aloud, giving instructions to his demonic powers to focus all efforts on this "gift" without measure, "If free will is what God wishes, then free will is what we shall exploit!"

This strategy will prove to be most effective.

Back in the city of Adam, at the tent of congregation, Adam finishes his teachings. Pausing momentarily and looking into all the faces of his family, Adam slowly turns his face upward to the Heavens and begins to speak a simple prayer.

As his humble request rises before the heavenly throne, the heart of God is moved with compassion. While Adam speaks from the very deepest part of his being, God is pleased and remembers the time in Eden's Garden before the fall, when He could walk in the cool of the day with both the man and the woman. God, looking intensely into the glistening eyes of His first created human being Adam, longs for that lost relationship to be restored.

From His Sovereign throne, God looks more than 1,500 years into the future. What He sees is like a shroud of darkness and corruption on a global scale. Every intention and every thought of man's heart had become only evil continually. This grieves the heart of God so much that He is sorry He has made man on the earth.

God is stirred in righteous anger, not against what He has created, but against the one who is truly responsible for all corruption. It is Satan who is the very seed of all sin itself. Springing forth from that single seed, the resulting plague of sinful rebellion has caused such widespread corruption that the entire earth now appears as sin continually to Almighty God.

Peering deeper into the midst of this fallen creation, God sees one shining star of righteousness piercing the ever increasing shroud of darkness.

There is still one whose faith remains true.

Turning His attention back to the present events at the tent of the congregation, God listens as Adam closes his humble prayer with a simple request, "Our God, in a land where sin seemingly abounds, may Your grace abound much more; may Your merciful hand be continually upon my family; and may Your will be done on earth as it is in Heaven."

Through the process of time, humans expand further into the north and south, moving eastward and to the west also as they continue to multiply and cover the face of the earth. Having learned to survive, they are now thriving upon this earth that God had created. It was the original intention and will of God that men from Adam forward would fill the earth and subdue it. Earth was created to be the perfect habitat for all humanity and the perfect place for the close personal relationship that God desired to enjoy with all human beings. However, just as God had foreseen in the day of Adam, the wickedness of all humanity has been carefully cultivated by the originator of sin himself.

The produce from one single seed of sin has truly abounded much fruit of disobedience and pure wickedness, even the earth itself became corrupted. No longer are men remorseful of their sins, no more cries of repentance are heard rising before the Holy and Righteous God.

Where there is no repentance of sin, there can be no forgiveness of sin.

With a personal relationship no longer possible, God in His righteousness passes judgement. Destruction of all wicked flesh upon the earth is the necessary verdict.

As God speaks this devastating result, in His great heart of love there is a promise of hope. God, remembering His own Words from the beginning, will provide salvation to all who will freely receive His Gift.

God has many Holy attributes but the first is fundamental: God cannot lie, and the second is principle: God keeps all of His promises.

God, in His eternal sovereignty, has preserved one shining light still present in this world filled with darkness. Remembering the prayer of Adam, now more than 1,500 years in earth's past, God is moved with great love and compassion. All Heaven now stands to witness as God, raising His Right Hand of power, makes a covenant promise to all creation, "*Wherever sin abounds, most assuredly My grace shall much more abound.*"

Circulating throughout this inhabited world is a story that is rapidly approaching mythical status. Most of the human population consider it to be a fable, or if true, highly exaggerated. Even so, as if carried to every corner of the land by some unseen herald, this story continues to spread as rapidly as does the evil intentions of men's hearts and minds.

People from all areas of the inhabited world come to see the origin of this great tale. Some come for entertainment and others to jeer and ridicule, but all come out of curiosity.

It is a fantastic story about a questionable old man whose message and reason seems as ridiculously unbelievable, as does his massive wooden project. This direct descendant from the household of Adam has continued to follow in the teachings past down from his forefathers and is faithfully teaching and leading his family in wor-shipping and serving the One True God.

One faithful man and his family will soon become mankind's only beacon of hope for salvation from the inevitable flood of God's coming judgement. He alone has found grace in the eyes of the Lord, and together with his family, hope for a new beginning.

Notes

Dear Reader,

Do you ever feel like something is missing from your life? Like an empty void has swallowed some vital part your life?

If you do not know the Lord Jesus Christ on a personal level, that is the first problem that needs your immediate attention. The Bible says that a life without Jesus Christ is a life that is "*dead in trespasses and sins*." (Ephesians 2:1)

If you have read the story within this book, you recall how in the beginning God made everything, including Man.

At the start, God provides the perfect world for the perfect relationship He desired with Mankind.

Having only one commandment to be kept, only one fruit to avoid, by their own choice, the first two humans fail to remain obedient.

On the day they disobey God and eat of the forbidden fruit, the consequences of sin became a reality: *"In the day that you eat of it, you shall surely die."* (Genesis 2:17)

Not only physical death, but spiritual death, a helpless separation from God.

The Bible continues to explain the full ramifications of this first sin: *"Therefore, just as through one man sin entered the world, and death through sin, and thus, death spread to all men, because all sinned."* (Romans 5:12)

Again, it is written in the Bible, *"As it is written: There is none righteous, no, not one; There is none who understands; There is none who seeks after God. They have all turned aside; They have together become unprofitable; There is none who does good, no, not one."* (Romans 3:10-12)

It is not merely about all the sins you commit, but about the Sin Nature you inherited from the first human couple. *"For all have sinned and fall short of the glory of God."* (Romans 3:23)

The results of sin are Death: Physically and Spiritually, and if you die without Jesus Christ as your Savior, Eternal death separated from God in the awful torment of the place called Hell.

But there is Hope.

Jesus, God in the flesh, came into this world not to further condemn it, but *"that the world through Him might be Saved."* (John 3:17) *"For God so loved the world that He gave His only begotten Son, that whosoever believes in Him should not perish but have everlasting life."* (John 3:16)

God leaves the choice up to you. Do you hear His voice tenderly calling through these scriptures?

He wants to breathe new life into you. Jesus called this New Life being "Born Again." He also said to Nicodemus, *"...except a man be born again, he cannot see the kingdom of God."*

As the Holy Spirit of God pleads with you, repent of your sins and turn to God by placing your Faith in the Lord Jesus Christ.

God made a Promise *"that if you will confess with your mouth the Lord Jesus Christ and believe in your heart that God has raised Him from the dead, You Shall Be Saved. For with the heart man believes unto righteousness, and with the mouth confession is made unto salvation."* (Romans 10:9,10)

When you turn your heart and life over to God, that once empty void will be eternally filled with the very Holy Spirit of God Himself. God will be to you as Father, and you will become His Child.

You will be freed from the penalty of death, for *"whom the Son has set free, is free indeed."* (John 8:36)

There will be *"no more condemnation to those who are in Christ Jesus."* (Romans 8:1)

You will be redeemed, justified and set apart: *"Sealed until the day of redemption."* (Ephesians 4:30)

You can rejoice in this great truth, *"that whosoever believes in Him shall not perish but shall have eternal life."* (John 3:16b)

If you desire this Free gift of Salvation, please pray sincerely in your own words, something similar to this:

> *Dear Lord, I now realize that I am a sinner and that you died for me. I repent of my sin, and ask you now to come into my heart, forgive me, save me, and take me to Heaven to be with you forever when I die. Thank you, Lord, for Saving Me.*
>
> *By your grace, I commit my New Life to you and will follow in the ways and teachings of Jesus.*
>
> *I pray in Jesus name, Amen.*

If you have prayed with all sincerity and have decided to trust Jesus Christ as your Savior, please contact us to receive your New Believer's gift:

Mail to:

Heartsway
2810 Middlebrook Pike
Knoxville, TN. 37921

Email: pastor@heartsway.church